Developing Environmental Education in the Curriculum

Edited by Steve Goodall

David Fulton Publishers
London

David Fulton Publishers Ltd
2 Barbon Close, London WC1N 3JX

First published in Great Britain by
David Fulton Publishers 1994

Note: The right of Steve Goodall to be identified as the editor of this work has been
asserted by him in accordance with the Copyright, Designs and Patents Act 1988.

Copyright © David Fulton Publishers Ltd

British Library Cataloguing in Publication Data

A catalogue record for this book is available from the British Library

ISBN 1-85346-322-1

Typeset by Textype Typesetters, Cambridge
Printed in Great Britain by BPC Books and Journals, Exeter

Contents

Contributors

Patrick Bailey	Consultant in Education and Trustee of the Geographical Association
Jeffrey Best	Course Leader, Environmental Science, Nene College, Northampton
David Blake	Advisory Teacher for English, Spencer Centre, Northampton
Terry Bull	Lecturer in Education, University of Trent, Nottingham
David Cain	Advisory Teacher for Mathematics, Spencer Centre, Northampton
Wasyl Cajkler	Lecturer in Education, University of Leicester
Issy Cole-Hamilton	Children's Rights Development Unit, London
Mike Cross	Lecturer, St Martin's College, Lancaster
Ian Curtis	Inspector for Primary Education, Northamptonshire
Ian Duffell	Industrial Fellow, Centre for Citizenship in Education Studies, University of Leicester
Janet Edwards	Deputy Director, Centre for Citizenship Studies in Education, University of Leicester
Steve Goodall	Headteacher, Old Stratford County Primary School
Linda Hargreaves	Lecturer in Education, University of Leicester
Jennifer Harrison	Lecturer in Education, University of Leicester
Bob Hopkins	Advisory Teacher, Northamptonshire Computer Education Centre
Tina Jarvis	Lecturer in Education, University of Leicester
David Kerr	Lecturer in Education, University of Leicester
Neil Kitson	Lecturer in Education, University of Leicester
Tony Lawson	Lecturer in Education, University of Leicester
Mark Lofthouse	Senior Lecturer in Education, University of Leicester
Marcus Lyon	Teacher, Roade Comprehensive School
Ros McCulloch	Lecturer in Education, University of Leicester
Terry Mortimer	Teacher, Nicholas Hawksmoor C.P. School, Towcester, Northamptonshire
Sue Paice	Pocket Parks Officer, Northamptonshire Countryside Services
Graham Robb	Headteacher, Lode Heath School, Solihull
Don Rowe	Director, The Citizenship Foundation, London
Alan Sutton	Lecturer in Education, University of Leicester
Drisc Wardle	Governor, Nicholas Hawksmoor C.P. School, Towcester
Martin Wenhan	Lecturer in Education, University of Leicester
Angela Wortley	Lecturer in Education, University of Leicester

Preface

The 1990 European elections in Great Britain are remembered for bringing environmental issues to the forefront of political debate. For a short time, it seemed as though the weight of public opinion would bring about political representation of telling numbers in the European Parliament.

There has also been some cause for optimism with the Earth Summit in Rio de Janeiro and a reduction in intensive agriculture in many European countries.

This book appears, however, at a time when the importance of Environmental Education has been reduced, like that of other cross-curricular themes, by the total lack of mention of them in the Dearing Review of the National Curriculum. If a school is to offer a curriculum which is broad, balanced and relevant, as the 1988 Education Reform Act insists, then teaching by subject would seem to be limited in its effectiveness to fulfil these requirements.

Thus not only does reference to cross-curricular themes give a school a start in demonstrating what 'added-on value' they are offering but it would seem to be a requirement in offering a curriculum which will serve children well.

In addition to these pragmatic reasons, there remains the central issue of the vital importance to the future of the human race of getting our solutions to environmental issues right in both the short and long term.

The editor has included three additional contributions to those in previous books in this series. The case study and relationships between schools and conservation bodies are important if Environmental Education in schools is going to take on practical investigation and development. The impact of Information Technology upon education was, in the editor's opinion very much underplayed in the National Curriculum. One may consider it as a subject in its own right, enabling pupils to do new things in schools. However, the editor suggests that its greatest impact is as a cross-curricular theme influencing all subjects and themes, enabling pupils to model the environment and ask that all-important question 'What would happen if?' Therefore there is an additional, sixth, theme.

Thanks are due to Mark Lofthouse, Janet Edwards and John Owens for their help and encouragement, as well as to all the contributors for their prompt delivery of articles.

CHAPTER 1

Introduction – Environmental Education

Steve Goodall

The articles in this book reflect the controversy and range of opinions and responses which environmental issues seem to elicit from commentators and teachers. Despite the lack of consensus regarding causes and remedial action, however, it seems clear that certain issues are now established which need consideration. Despite the lack of guidance about cross-curricular themes, and Environmental Education in particular, in the most recent reports on the National Curriculum, schools would do well to recognise the importance of such issues to their pupils. Pragmatically, teachers will be reluctant to abandon all their curriculum design efforts and investment in resources. They would be hard-pressed to do better than regard consideration of environmental education as evidence of 'added-on value' which would have practical benefit to both pupils' long-term prospects and a school faced with OFSTED inspection.

Environmental education challenges, as well as relates to the other cross-curricular themes. The advice offered to schools by the National Curriculum Council in *Curriculum Guidance 7* is clear. It is excellent in showing common study links with other themes but is not explicit enough in stating where attention might be focussed in order to obtain the clearest picture of what causes environmental problems. However, if environmental education is to be effective in raising awareness of the issues, one must identify, as unambiguously as possible, what those issues are. These issues may be summarised as:

—the growth of human activity;
—global warming and its energy implications;
—global food security;
—the population backlash;
—the information society.

(King and Schneider, 1991a)

There has been a huge increase in the range and amount of human activity since the turn of the century which makes increasingly large demands upon raw materials, energy sources and human resources. By compounding population numbers with average per capita consumption, one is able to obtain a rough indication of the totality of human activity. King and Schneider estimate a forty-fold increase over the century to date. (King and Schneider, 1991b) Human lifestyles which threaten the ozone layer are being curtailed as public awareness rises and demands action by producers.

Although the issue is complex, the 'greenhouse effect' appears to constrain the extension of an economic approach to social organisation. The exact consequences of the heating of the earth's surface are still open to debate but there seems to be general agreement as to what the general trend is. The estimated rises in temperature caused by a doubling in carbon dioxide equilibrium concentrations is much greater than any alterations which have arisen through historical cyclic fluctuations. The effects are thought to be smaller at the equator and much greater at higher latitudes, altering thermal gradients, changing precipitation patterns, modifying climatic zones and thus changing agricultural viability.

Human activity which alters agricultural potential and removes fertile land for other purposes, such as mineral extraction or transport, may be linked in its effect with a rising world population. Technically, one may be able to grow sufficient food to support a population of twenty billion, but this is to discount the huge demands on energy which would be needed to supply sufficient fresh water to support the enterprise. Moreover the agricultural revolution, which has produced food surpluses, has not led to the elimination of hunger. Even in countries such as India, where the food is being produced in reasonable proximity to the hungry, problems of malnutrition and famine persist. Transport difficulties, from surplus-producing regions such as North America, to deficit areas, and the reliance of modern agriculture upon energy-expensive methods of producing fertilisers and weedkillers question the future of a surplus in food supply. There has also been a recent and dramatic fall in food reserves following the droughts since 1989 in North America. Harvests fell by 31% in the USA and 27% in Canada.

Large demographic changes are to be expected in the industrialized countries caused by their ageing populations and falling birthrates. Automation and increasing productivity may generate sufficient national product to maintain living standards with a reduced workforce, but a substantial burden will be placed upon pension and health care systems. Additionally, adjustments will have to be made to educational systems as the success of family-planning attitudes works its way through the population. Differences between countries in the opportunities for individuals to succeed could cause population movements. Conditions of tyranny and oppression and population pressures may well cause irreversible migratory waves North and West. The populations of rich countries will have to prepare themselves to accept the reality of the need for cooperation to reduce, significantly, economic disparity. The development of an information or post-industrial society is a major result of, and cause of, global changes. It is possible to communicate wise, constructive developments which could benefit the whole of humankind. It is equally possible to communicate racism, greed, envy and tyranny. Technological innovation has always influenced society's behaviour patterns. A society after the Industrial Revolution had significantly different organisational and behavioural beliefs than its agricultural predecessor. An increase in information technology and automation may produce new products, industries and markets but one has yet to see whether it will produce jobs to match the level of employment of the industrial society it overtakes.

These issues are interlinked and it makes little sense to tackle them individually. Although this linkage makes any study complex, it does highlight the need for educationalists to begin to think on an international scale rather than just in localised contexts.

Environmental education has close links with the other four cross-curricular themes, sharing many of the same features of investigative study skills and bodies of knowledge. Pupils may research original and secondary sources, set up simulations, reach conclusions and discuss the validity of their ideas. The five themes share the possibilities for promoting the discussion of values and beliefs, extending knowledge and understanding, encouraging practical activities and decision-making and providing opportunities for pupils to make positive contributions to their community's way of life.

Yet the human race is faced with the actualities of increasing air and water pollution, the 'greenhouse effect' and global warming, the increasing destruction of rain forests and its consequences for weather patterns. On all continents the deserts advance steadily and daily the extinction of species occurs whose role in world ecology has never been assessed. The importance of the environment has been forcefully set out by Bellamy:

—a need for a diverse genetic bank, especially to ensure continued food production;
—all life depends ultimately upon food production by plants which use the sun's energy;
—diverse habitats are little studied and may contain unknown sources of medicine;
—clean air and water are finite resources;
—energy sources are finite;
—humans seem to need wild places for their spiritual and physical well-being.

(Quoted in Goodall, 1993a)

The finite nature of the world's resources and fine balance between the existence and collapse of delicate ecologies has never been more clearly

4

brought to our attention.

Obvious as these environmental issues may appear to be, this is still an area of considerable debate and contention, especially among those practising scientists and philosophers of scientific methodology who adhere to Karl Popper's belief that Science is a discipline which continually tries to prove its ideas to be wrong. His methodology is one of conjecture and refutation. But Popper is concerned with how scientists ought to behave and not so much with how they do behave. (Castri, 1990) Whilst in Physics a number of hypotheses have withstood the rigorous testing of time and intellect to attain the status of theories, in Biology many hypotheses have not yet attained the same status through the rigorous accumulation of data. For example, while Newton's Theory of Gravity is now accepted (though the Graviton, the particle responsible for carrying the force of gravity remains a theoretical notion), Darwin's Theory of Evolution still evokes rather greater debate in scientific circles.

There is the opportunity for educationalists to concentrate upon fundamentally important issues for the human race. One must recognise that only the most impartial and rigorous of approaches to questions about the survival of the human race allows for useful conclusions to be reached. It is not satisfactory for challenges to current ideas to be met by the introduction of auxiliary hypotheses which are designed to meet the criticism. This methodology merely allows a hypothesis to survive a little longer despite mounting evidence that it is inadequate or even wrong. It is not a methodology of which Popper would approve.

'Global warming' is likely to involve a number of complex, interconnected factors. One may hypothesise that one recognises a particular product by its logo. However, no amount of empirical observation will overcome the 'Problem of Induction' which always prevents one from saying that the product will always be recognised by that symbol. One observation of a product without that trademark is enough to falsify the hypothesis. With an issue like 'global warming' an observation that thousands of hectares of rain forest can be seen burning everyday from space satellites may be an indicator that such production of carbon dioxide causes 'global warming'. The discovery of high levels of carbon dioxide in factory or traffic emissions does not disqualify forest burning as a factor. We may be dealing with a multi-faceted network of human activities which have to be unravelled. The National Curriculum Council advice:

> ...environmental education is the subject of considerable debate and that there is no clear consensus about many of the issues. (NCC, 1990a)

is correct in its caution and echoes similar difficulties to be found in issues connected with Citizenship.

In May, 1988 the Resolution of the Council and the Ministers of Education of the Council of the European Community stated that:

> The objective of environmental education is to increase the public awareness of the

---

problems in this field, as well as possible solutions, and to lay the foundations for a fully informed and active participation of the individual in the protection of the environment and the prudent and rational use of natural resources.

(NCC, 1990b)

The Resolution suggested some principles which might inform environmental education:

—the environment as the common heritage of mankind;
—the common duty of maintaining, protecting and improving the quality of the environment, as a contribution to the protection of human health and the safeguarding of the ecological balance;
—the need for a prudent and rational utilisation of resources;
—the way in which each individual can, by his own behaviour, particularly as a consumer, contribute to the protection of the environment.

(NCC, 1990b)

Even here a subjective vocabulary is used: e.g. 'possible solutions', the 'quality' of the environment, and 'rational' utilisation of resources. These are, and have to be, political decisions which carry difficult, moral and value-ridden meanings. Effective environmental education accepts these problems and recognises the richness of them as sources of moral debate and development. The knowledge content of Environmental Education as suggested by the National Curriculum Council (NCC, 1990c) is reasonably straightforward provided teachers are able to use contemporary findings and developments. The skills of communication, numeracy, study, problem-solving, information technology, and personal and social interaction are broadly shared with the other cross-curricular themes. The positive attitudes to be encouraged include:

—appreciation of, and care and concern for the environment and for other living things;
—independence of thought on environmental issues;
—a respect for the beliefs and opinions of others;
—a respect for evidence and rational argument;
—tolerance and open-mindedness.

(NCC, 1990d)

It is important to note that there is a degree of selfishness here as each individual tries to survive or avoid censure by community norms or national laws of equality. Education about the environment, its climate, geology, water, resources, living systems and human activities can only provide a common framework within which the moral and values debate takes place. One cannot teach about the environment without ascribing values to the existence and desirability of certain kinds of environment. Pupils may debate how to ensure the best immediate and future use of the environment.

They may consider possible solutions to environmental problems taking into account conflicting interests and making informed choices. In doing so they are taking part in a moral and political debate.

One effective way of ensuring that the issues are fully identified is through practical, firsthand enquiry, research and investigation. In this respect one is fortunate that local environmental issues are so often a small-scale echo of much larger, global issues. Primary school conservation projects reflect major conservation programmes across the globe. Suggestions by pupils about traffic control around their school relate to national issues of road building, pollution and the use of finite resources such as land and fuel. Initiatives within schools to deal with vandalism, graffiti and the design of and access to buildings touch directly upon wider questions of how society might be governed, respect for the law and community relationships.

These connections reflect questions and assumptions back upon the possible solutions to environmental problems. However, these solutions are likely to depend upon how pupils see themselves in terms of their citizenship. Their responsibilities for the environment may be defined by whether they consider themselves as citizens of a community, country or international group like Europe. (Goodall, 1993b) As pupils search for answers and develop their perspectives and wider understanding so their own solutions to environmental problems may also change. Pupils' ideas may challenge a school's or their parents' assumptions. These aspects need sensitive consideration for there are no right answers and teachers must be prepared to be challenged by pupils' reactions and suggestions.

The complex and transient nature of environmental issues precludes any definitive statement of how those problems might be solved. Teachers should encourage pupils to seek their own logical solutions and to examine, impartially and critically, the solutions currently offered. We have to do this against the background of two, interrelated phenomena. Moral awareness has been lessened by the questioning of ethical structures and role models as an increasingly heterogeneous society gains access to more information. There may be a tendency to retreat from the daunting scale of global change. For example there has been a resurgence of political instability in various countries which has moved towards narrow nationalism or individualism.

At the same time the information society has enabled a progressively more complete awareness of environmental issues and problems to take hold of the public imagination. While expectations for solutions and research into possibilities are encouraged, the mass of information, uncritically presented can be overwhelming. Issues may be clouded, leading to repetition or compounding of errors. Spiritual, ethical and moral dimensions which redefine the quality of the environment and of human life should not be a matter of indifference, irrelevance or scorn but a vital ingredient in the search for a new humanity.

Schools could try to make sure that the learning opportunities they offer are a part of that essential process whereby solutions to environmental problems are found and implemented. Ideally every pupil ought to participate in seeking and defining the 'right' or best solutions among the many possibilities. This must mean appreciating the complexity of the network of issues to be considered. Further, pupils might be enabled to recognise that positive improvements to the environment can only be rooted in the motives and value systems that govern behaviour. Indeed the behaviour of nations, their alliances and society structures, in general reflects the behaviour patterns exhibited by their individual members. It is unlikely that any single action at government level will alter the environment for the better. It is more likely that it will require many individual acts, at the local level, in order to bring about significant change. If every individual were to buy ozone-friendly products, burn less fuel and join recycling schemes then producers would have to change. As consumers each individual does not have to accept what is on offer but can make demands upon the providers of goods and services. With the privilege of belonging to a relatively advantaged society comes the responsibility of seeking solutions to environmental and social problems.

In 1989, some forty decision-makers in Colorado came to realise the importance of global–local interaction. In cooperation between the United Nations Conference on Environment and Development and the Club of Rome, further national initiatives have continued in order to foster the message of local action. These initiatives in some thirty countries on five continents advocate local individual interactions with a view to transforming citizens from being inactive and isolated persons into becoming aware human beings ready to take cohesive action.

As empowered citizens we could know a lot about the environmental issues we face by using the information systems technology has provided. This does not make it easier to understand the issues or make decisions about proposed solutions. One has therefore to learn how to proceed in the face of uncertainty. Political decisions often have to be taken when the possible outcomes or contributory factors are not completely identified. As individuals or as members of institutions, one is increasingly asked to adopt attitudes and approaches of greater flexibility and adaptability. One real challenge is to make links of common understanding between the language and concepts of economics, morality and environmental issues. One might adopt environmental and moral considerations in the assessment of economic analysis; or take account of economic viewpoints in approaching environmental problems. Careful definition of the environmental issues and their causes and the kind of economics being used is needed. More effective ways of integrating environmental issues with macro- and micro-economic perspectives have to be found.

Citizens involved in local initiatives who are concerned about future generations and their well-being would have to balance and reconcile present

8

and future problems and values with needs. The creation of a sustainable world system suggests that profligate lifestyles need to be diminished by decelerating consumption of finite resources. An ethical imperative also requires one to alleviate poverty wherever possible. Current ethical decisions are largely undefined, diffuse reactions against environmental ills such as pollution or selfish exploitation of resources. In some countries, a business-based system of regulation offers some protection against various forms of malpractice, but local action based upon ethical consideration deserves to strengthen systems of regulation. Practitioners in the business of industry, commerce, service or conservation would then have to accept a higher degree of social and environmental responsibility in their own and consumers' long-term interests.

The articles presented in this book offer a rich source of ideas, examples and discussions. They will be an aid to educationalists who wish to begin to explore the issues more thoroughly. The considerations are contemporary ones which should enable pupils' educational experience to be relevant to the real world. Otherwise one may take refuge in having a curriculum which is sentimentalized or cliché-ridden. Quite rightly, HMI have already pointed out the biased nature of some curricula, which simply label all industrial and technological activity as environmentally, 'bad'.

An ethical perspective of international relations cannot evolve unless it has a positive effect at a national, community and individual level. Schools could help foster positive attitudes on the part of pupils towards being involved in sound local initiatives which promote care for the environment at a local level while echoing global issues. The development of effective strategies to deal with environmental issues requires research into, and an understanding of, the real causes of the problems. This would be more easily done if pupils were encouraged to consider local problems and become involved in local initiatives to solve them. Schools would thus play an essential formative role in the development of aware citizens who would be equipped to tackle the complex environmental issues they will face in the future.

References

Castri, J. (1990) *Paradigms Lost.* New York: Scribners (pp.32–33).
Goodall, S.C. (1993a) 'Environmental education' in Edwards, J. and Fogelman, K. (eds.) *Developing Citizenship in the Curriculum.* London: David Fulton Publishers (p40; (b) pp.39–42).
King, A. and Schneider, B. (1991a) *The First Global revolution: A Report by the Council of The Club of Rome – the World twenty years after 'The Limits of Growth'.* London: Simon and Schuster (pp.33–53; (b) p.34).
NCC (1990a) *Curriculum Guidance 7: Environmental Education.* York: National Curriculum Council (p.1; (b) p.3; (c) p.4; (d) p.24).

CHAPTER 2

Environmental Education and other Cross-Curricular Themes

ECONOMIC AND INDUSTRIAL UNDERSTANDING

Alan Sutton

> 'The extinction of animals is an emotional outrage to all sensitive human beings but it's hard to put a price on such losses in a world where economics is the principal rule of human behaviour.'
>
> (Buckley, 1992)

Economic literacy is arguably a key requirement of the whole curriculum for young people if they are to understand the causes, effects and ways of tackling environmental problems whether they be on a local or global scale. Economic perspectives should be an integral part of any discussion of environmental issues alongside other perspectives such as, political, social and technological since 'students should be encouraged to examine and interpret the environment from a variety of perspectives'. (NCC, 1990) The need to examine the significance of the economic dimension is important for a variety of reasons. Economic factors are a contributory and often major cause of environmental problems. Some of these environmental problems are more serious and concentrated in their effects because of economic factors. Technological solutions to environmental issues are sometimes available but not taken up because of cost factors. The unequal distribution of wealth between the 'North' and 'South' has an influence on the scale of environmental problems and possible solutions. There is a growing recognition that the misuse of the environment has economic costs and an acceptance that when cost benefits are weighed up, only a portion of degraded land can be satisfactorily rehabilitated. Finally there is a growing acceptance of the need for sustainable development in which conservation and development are planned together.

How can the integration of EIU into Environmental Education be planned for ?

Both EIU and Environmental Education are important cross-curricular themes in the National Curriculum. In order to aid teachers in planning the curriculum, guidance for Environmental Education draws on a model developed in the 1970s, 'education about, through, and for the environment'. In *Curriculum Guidance 7*, teachers are presented with a list of environmental topics for guidance but teaching Environmental Education may best be approached as a series of issues many of which are controversial and in which the importance of economic literacy is a key to understanding. How can EIU be integrated into environmental education particularly in those subjects in which the environmental problems are an important part of syllabuses, particularly Geography and Science? In a consideration of any of the major environmental problems there are a number of questions which can be investigated in relation to these four dimensions.

Planning the integration of EIU into Environmental Education: a conceptual model

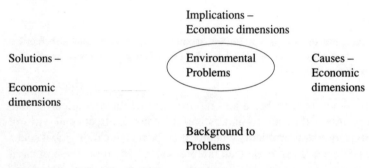

They are:
(1) What are the indicators of the problem?
(2) How is the problem perceived?
(3) Where is the problem occurring?
(4) What is the scale and rate of the problem?
(5) What are the causes?
(6) What are the implications?
(7) What measures can be taken to avoid, mitigate or rehabilitate?
(8) What is economically feasible?

A growing interest in global environmental/developmental issues

Not until the 1960s was there anything but patchy interest in the environmental dimensions of development. In 1972, the UN Conference on Human Environment in Stockholm was instrumental in bringing countries together to consider the future of the earth. Between 1973 and 1985, there were a number of studies expressing environmental/developmental concern notably the Brandt Report in 1980. In the late 1980s, the World Commission on Environment and Development (The Brundtland Report) marked a issues with the move to sustainable development. There is now a general acceptance that there are a series of major global environmental problems. These are:

—global warming;
—damage to the ozone layer;
—deforestation, particularly of the tropical rain forest;
—acid rain;
—soil erosion;
—desertification;
—the threat to endangered species of plants and animals.

How significant are these problems?

Each of these global problems are characterized by their scale and complexity, their interdependence, the threat that they pose to the planet and the fact that they require international cooperation to tackle them. There are some clear trends: land is being lost from production at an alarming rate; global levels of carbon dioxide and the ozone levels already give cause for concern; the loss of genetic resources as species become extinct is serious and accelerating; the effects of toxic chemical and other pollutants are significant and increasing; the problem of soil erosion is potentially the most serious form of resource depletion. The problems are world wide and particularly affect the South. Some developing countries appear to be trapped in a downward spiral of interlinked ecological and economic decline. Sub Saharan Africa and Amazonia are often cited as particularly prone to environmental/developmental problems but there are many other areas affected in both the North and South.

What are the economic causes of environmental problems?

There are several explanations of environmental degradation from the environmental development literature which involve economic considerations. One consequence of the economics of production is that entrepreneurs tend to maximise profits in the short term possibly incurring degradation and then invest all or part of their profits elsewhere. External factors acting on production systems can cause or contribute to environmental degradation, notably world market forces, neocolonialism and the action of multinationals. The terms of international trade are seen by many economists as having caused increased economic dependency and indebtedness in developing nations. Many developing countries spend much of their revenue repaying foreign debt and consequently are less able to afford conservation measures. Timber, minerals and land are ruthlessly exploited to try to generate desperately needed foreign exchange. The unequal distribution of wealth between the North and the South is an important underlying factor accounting for a high consumer demand in the more affluent North, putting pressure on the South to develop their resources. The search for profits and the desire to maintain living standards in the North is resulting in a threat to several endangered species notably the tiger, the whale, the elephant and the dolphin. For instance recent evidence suggests that the Blue Whale population has declined to 450 in the whole of the southern hemisphere. The killing of the whale is not an economic necessity for Norwegian fishermen but whale meat is a traditional part of the Japanese diet!

What are the economic implications of these environmental problems?

All of these environmental problems have an adverse effect on production, standards of living, quality of life, sometimes including life and death. They have both direct and indirect costs. Soil erosion results in a decline in crop productivity and the indirect costs such as the silting of reservoirs result in an associated loss of water, power and increased flooding. The direct costs are vast, the indirect costs are considerable. For instance in Ethiopia, soil erosion caused by decline in forest cover cuts agricultural production by a million tons a year. Some have local and distant effects; river flooding in Bangladesh, partly caused by the removal of the forest cover in the upper reaches of the Brahmaputra, annually affects 20% of the country ruining crops and causing loss of life. Desertification is one of the most serious problems facing the world and the annual loss of land world wide to significant desertification is an area larger than Belgium. It was calculated that, world wide, dry land degradation in 1987 cost 26 billion US dollars a year in lost agricultural production. It is estimated that acid rain costs the German economy 28 billion dollars a year. Crude estimates of the value of crop losses due to acid deposition are calculated to be costing Europe 500 million US dollars a year.

How can the problems be tackled?

From the late 1960s, there was a movement for those involved in development to encompass a consideration of environmental issues. The concept of ecologically sustainable development seems to have been first voiced in the late 1960s. Later the world conservation strategy in 1980 and more recently the Brundtland Report (1987) and the Pearce Report (1989) gave the concept wider publicity. This approach demands an anticipate/avoid rather than a react and cure approach to development. It demands that the question be asked, 'Is it ever acceptable to engage in actions that reduce the potential of future generations to meet their needs?' (Barrow) Distinctions have been made between sustainable development and sustainable exploitation. Whereas the latter is about maintaining a dynamic equilibrium between production and consumption, sustainable development is linked to economic growth. It has been suggested that sustainable development should ensure that the poor have access to secure livelihoods and that the distribution of wealth does not become more unequal. The main problem in controlling these problems is the cost factor. It is recognized that the Third World cannot afford to pay for the environmental policies which the rest of the world demands, yet we still have a situation where net transfers from the South to the North exceed 50 billion dollars a year largely because of interest payment on debts. Some of this money could be used to fund 'debt swap approaches' which already have been used to combat deforestation in the tropics. For some environmental problems, the technology is available but the economic costs are considered to be prohibitive. For instance, future power stations in the UK (a significant cause of acid rain in Western Europe) will have better pollution control which will reduce emissions by 90%. Most of the world's desertification problems could be reversed with present available technology but at a cost.

> It would not be surprising if most teachers, primary and secondary, find themselves with too little time to devote to the issues of coherence within cross curricular provision and between cross curricular provision and the foundation subjects.

> (Hargreaves)

This chapter has focused on the relationship between economic and industrial understanding and environmental education. It is argued that a basic economic literacy with an understanding of economic concepts such as opportunity, costs, profit, supply and demand, terms of international trade, global interdependence and sustainable development are essential to understand the background to, causes, effects and possible strategies to tackle environmental problems. A balanced treatment of any environmental problem should ensure that these dimensions and themes and concepts inform planning in the secondary curriculum.

References

Barrow, C.J. (1991) *Land Degradation*. Cambridge: Cambridge University Press.

Buckley, R. (ed.) (1992) *Amazonia. An Ecological Crisis. Understanding Global Issues*. Cheltenham: European School Books Publishing Limited.

Hargreaves, D.H. (1991) 'Coherence and Manageability: Reflections on the National Curriculum and cross curricular provision' *The Curriculum Journal*, **Vol.2**, No.1.

NCC (1991) *Curriculum Guidance 7: Environmental Education*. York: National Curriculum Council.

Palmer, J. (1989) The National Curriculum – Framework for Opportunity. The Location of an Environmental Education as a Cross Curricular Issue. NAEE Occasional Paper 13.

Pearce, D., Markandya, A. and Barbier, E. (1989) *Blueprint for a Green Economy*. London: Earthscan Publications.

World Commission on Environment and Development (1987) *Our Common Future. Report of the World Commission on Environment and Development (The Brundtland Report)*. Oxford: Oxford University Press.

WWF UK (1980) *World Conservation Strategy: Living Resources Conservation for Sustainable Development*. London: IUCN, UNEP, WWF, UK.

WWF UK (1991) *Caring for the Earth: A Strategy for Sustainable Living*. London: IUCN, UNEP, WWF, UK.

14

HEALTH EDUCATION

Jennifer Harrison

One common characteristic of the cross-curricular themes is that they can all focus on controversial concerns, and therefore there is considerable overlap within topics such as 'population growth' and 'food production'. Like other themes, the curriculum area of health education has much to offer environmental education.

People's relationships with the environment are interwoven with their personal health and lifestyles. In terms of environmental education it is important to remember these are global relationships involving a complex network of interdependent systems, (ecological, physical and chemical, geological), in which human societies and institutions are components. Human populations make enormous changes to the earth, influencing, by their dependence on particular agrarian economies, the disappearance of important habitats, and bringing about the extinction of many species. Human population growth has a two-fold effect: it fuels both environmental destruction and human destitution. We know that nearly a quarter of humanity lives in poverty, unable to meet basic needs for food, shelter and clothing. We know that there is a relationship between high fertility and high mortality. Contraceptive help is crucial in many countries and yet, only slowly, is the concept of sustainable growth and development gaining ground.

One of the dangers inherent in environmental education is that pupils become so overwhelmed by the enormity of the world's problems that they lapse into apathy or cynical resignation. Too often the environmental problem is presented as the determinant of the human response. For example, increased incidence of UV light from the sun is associated with increased incidence of skin cancer. By examining the power of people to alter the environment through changes in attitude and by concerted effort, the thinning of the ozone layer can be examined in terms of assessing aerosol usage, using CFC free products, and developing policies to limit their use. All of these approaches are within reach of the 'environmentally friendly' school.

There are a number of curriculum approaches which can be adopted to promote health education. The essentially individualistic approach taken in *Curriculum Guidance 5* provides for health education which is about bodily functions and personal growth, and which has an emphasis on knowledge, attitudes and behaviour of individuals. In examining the balance between people and their immediate environment, the nine components of the health education curriculum provides numerous opportunities for exploring ideas central to local as well as global environmental issues.

In *Curriculum Guidance 3* reference is made 'to the importance of the spirit and ethos of the school'. The aims, attitudes, values and procedures of a school are fundamental to the success of any health education programme, and profoundly influence the extent to which individual awareness, responsibility and personal decision-making develop. Therefore the concept of the 'health promoting school' (Harrison and Edwards, 1994) does provide an opportunity to:

take a wider view including all aspects of the life of the school and its relationship with the community e.g. developing a school as a caring community.

(Young and Williams, 1989)

Teachers who can create a classroom climate in which levels of self-esteem are high, in which there is respect for individual needs, opinions and differences, and in which there are open and trusting relationships, will encourage learning about health and, in turn, enhance aspects of environmental education. Like other cross-curricular themes, environmental education involves focussing on a wide range of concepts, processes and perspectives. The learning environments, within and beyond the classroom, need to reflect the attitude and values which the school's environmental programme is trying to cultivate.

Pupils' involvement in their own surroundings is important in both health and environmental education. According to the Learning Through Landscapes Trust many school playgrounds:

are hideous wastelands, following years of institutional neglect and short-term planning: the most under-used educational resource in the country.

(Learning Through Landscapes, 1992).

The Trust is tackling the problem of transforming such school sites. The school grounds provide many opportunities for pupils taking responsibility, for example, by becoming involved in setting up and maintaining a pond or a wild life area and maintaining records of birds, plants, butterflies, and so on. Such direct experience provides a rich opportunity for young people to care for that environment and to seek to improve it.

One of the components of *Curriculum Guidance 5*, *'Psychological Aspects of Health Education'*, emphasises mental health, emotional well-being and stress, and thus a 'health promoting school' can seek opportunities to address some of the same criteria as the 'green' school. This can be done by:

● Providing bright, cheerful, purposeful and welcoming displays to celebrate success and to provide a stimulus for learning and further achievements.
● Provision of signs that are supportive in tone and wording.
● Creating resource areas that are comfortable, well lit and well heated.
● Creating safe movement patterns, and places for pupils to keep warm and dry outside lesson times.

Overall an environment that is free of litter, graffiti and clutter, with pleasant eating and toilet arrangements and safe places for everyone's possessions, can provide pupils, in both the 'hidden' as well as the 'formal' curriculum, opportunity to acquire knowledge and understanding of factors affecting mental health and emotional well-being.

Another health component, 'Safety', provides pupils with the opportunity for:

> Acquisition of knowledge and understanding of safety in different environments...of skills and strategies...to maintain their personal safety and that of others.
>
> (NCC, 1990a)

A 'health promoting school' can sell 'dayglo' armbands to young pedestrians, and crash helmets to young cyclists as well as teach the Green Cross Code and offer the chance to participate in cycling proficiency schemes. Much can be done to extend pupils' awareness of road safety and personal responsibility. By using local road safety officers, material from RoSPA, and literature from police 'drink–driving' campaigns (with links to the health component 'Substance use and abuse'), issues like driver fatigue, stress, drug use and other distractions can be highlighted and linked to causes of accident. Pupils can be encouraged to think about risks and risk-taking, accident blackspots, weather hazards, and to learn about emergency first aid procedures.

Health and safety at work is also an environmental issue which has links with both health education and Personal and Social Education:

> The quality and safety of the environment in which working and learning takes place can have a profound effect on outcomes and should be of paramount importance to the managers of any establishment.
>
> (Baczala, 1992).

There are EC regulations concerning computer use and aspects of the work situation, such as the quality of the screen and basic ergonomics in the work situation. These regulations have arisen because of rising incidences of repetitive strain injury, eye strain, stress, VDU emissions and links to miscarriage during pregnancy. Pupils could consider to what extent ergonomically designed keyboards and 'mice' have helped to alleviate some of these health problems.

The health component 'Food and Nutrition' provides opportunities to consider the implications of there being just three species, wheat, rice and maize, which provide half the world's food. Another four species, potato, barley, sweet potato and cassava, bring the total to three quarters (Lean, 1990). Such dependence on few crops is dangerous to health, and disease spreads rapidly through mono-cultures, well-illustrated by the Irish potato famines of the 1840s which caused a fifth of the country's people to die. Human population growth and the need for increased food production are inextricably linked. Pupils can be taught to understand that successes in food production have benefited some societies with huge increases in productivity. However, there is also opportunity to consider whether we can afford the resultant losses of species.

Finally there is an important health component entitled 'Environmental Aspects of Health Education'. At Key Stage 4 the NCC guidance (NCC, 1990b) suggests pupils should:

> understand how legislation and political, social, economic and cultural decisions affect health;
> develop a commitment to the care and improvement of their own and other people's health, community and environment.

This opportunity for community action in health, raises pupils' awareness of environmental and political limits to health, but is clearly at odds with the individualistic approach taken in the rest of *Curriculum Guidance 5*. Good case study material for use in secondary schools has been offered by Baines (1990) who, for instance, allows pupils to reconcile the dilemma of making farming and conservation more compatible.

> Education for sustainability is a vital precondition for people's health and well-being for the future...We believe the foundations of sustainable development are built mainly on the way people think, the values they hold, and the decisions they make...
>
> (UNCED, 1992)

More ideas for the classroom can be found in Harrison (1993).

Thus health education for the environment provides a vital context for environmental education. It is clearly the responsibility of all teachers of health education to enable pupils to form opinions and to make decisions about the links between human activity and the environment.

References.

Baczala, K. (1992) *Towards a School Policy for Environmental Education: Environmental Audit*. London: National Association for Environmental Education.

Baines, J. (1990) *Finding Out...About Conservation and Development*. London: Hobsons Publishing.

Harrison, J. (1993) *Cross-curricular Theme Pack 3: Health Education*. Cambridge: Pearson Publishing.

Harrison, J. and Edwards, J. (1994) *Developing Health Education in the Curriculum*. London: David Fulton Publishers (Chapter 2).

Lean, J. (1990) *Atlas of the Environment*. London: Arrow Books.

Learning Through Landscapes Newsletter (Summer 1992) *Grounds for Examination: The Challenge of the Secondary School Site*. Winchester: Learning Through Landscapes Trust.

NCC (1990a) *Curriculum Guidance Document 5: Health Education*. York: National Curriculum Council (p.4; (b) p.20).

United Nations Conference on Environment and Development (UNCED) (1992) *Good Earth-Keeping: Education, Training and Awareness for a Sustainable Future*. New York: United Nations Environment Programme UNEP–UK.

18

Young, I. and Williams, T. (1989) *The Healthy School*. Edinburgh: Scottish Health Education Group/World Health Organisation (p.32).

CAREERS EDUCATION

Graham Robb

Environmental education in the curriculum is under threat as the cross-curricular themes have no mention in the Dearing Review of the National Curriculum. (Dearing, 1994) Geography, a major vehicle for Environmental Education, is no longer compulsory beyond Key Stage 3. Meanwhile Careers Education and Guidance is a theme that must be found time at Key Stages 3 and 4. Initiatives from the Employment Department and Department for Education confirm its role in the curriculum. All this is at a time when the employment climate and opportunities for young people can only be fully understood in global, ecological terms. The relationship between Environmental and Careers Education can be understood by considering the current provision in schools.

A pupil may experience Environmental Education as elements in many subjects and activities. The support for such a programme depends upon the views of the senior management team of a school and the professional enthusiasm of the staff. There may be a post of responsibility for an Environmental Education coordinator but it is rare that a school has this theme as a key element in its school brochure or gives it prominence in the annual report to parents. On the other hand, careers may have an explicit timetable, or at least a recognisable programme of input. This is supported by the Recording of Achievement process especially with the expansion of Youth Credits. Careers education and guidance is also given status in school by the activities of external agencies such as Careers Services and the priorities of the Training and Enterprise Councils. A school is likely to have a careers guidance post of responsibility with non-teaching time allocated for the work. They may have administrative support and attend meetings of senior management. The activities of the school, linked with industry, are likely to be given publicity as opportunities arise to do so. Despite this there is evidence that the provision of careers education and guidance in schools varies considerably. (Cleaton, 1987 and 1993) Indicators which may measure such provision are curriculum time, resources, qualified staff allocation, policy statements and evaluation systems. The proposition is offered that this patchiness exists because of a lack of understanding of the conceptual basis of careers education. One must examine the, often simplistic and unhelpful, concept of CEG in order to demonstrate a common framework of understanding for careers education and guidance and environmental education.

Principles of CEG

For some years the commonly used conceptual framework underlying careers education and guidance was summarised in the acronym **DOTS**:

- Decision-making;
- Opportunity awareness;
- Transition skills;
- Self-awareness.

Much curriculum innovation and development was based on DOTS, underpinned by *Careers Education from 5-16*. (HMI, 1988) The Education Reform Act 1988 made implicit the role of CEG by placing a statutory responsibility on schools to provide a broad and balanced curriculum which:

> promotes the spiritual, moral, cultural, mental and physical development of pupils at the school, and of society.' and 'prepares pupils for the opportunities and experiences of adult life.

Curriculum Guidance 6 (NCC, 1990) identified five components of CEG as follows:

> Careers Education, a planned programme in all four key stages;
> —Access to information.
> —Experience of work.
> —Access to individual guidance.
> —Recording Achievement.
> —Planning for the future.

While the statement of the components is a helpful one, some practitioners still prefer to base their curriculum thinking on DOTS because they feel it offers a clearer conceptual framework.

However there is an even more profound issue to be explored. The underlying purpose of careers education is crucial. Law (1992) identifies certain concept clusters relating to CEG:

> CEG can be based upon matching pupils to vacancies.
> There is the concept of enabling students to develop their awareness of self and be more self-directed in dealing with opportunities which arise.
> Directive work may be undertaken in which pupils are coached for the opportunities which are available.
> In networking pupils are taught to make the most of the networks available to them, whether through Record of Achievement interviews or community service.
> Finally there is the concept of educating, with a focus on learned behaviour.

In this last idea Law identifies learning taking place in four stages:

> gathering and organising impressions;
> checking and understanding points of view;
> dealing with problem-solving and decision-making processes;
> accepting responsibility in a situation for oneself and others.

A conceptual approach to CEG, which is based on 'educating', may provide the most helpful developmental pathway. Any other concept would seem insufficiently rigorous to allow young people to analyse the wider world.

The problem arises as to the extent to which these activities are an entitlement which all pupils should experience and how far they are experienced by self-selected groups. This is an issue of curriculum design.

CEG: An Environmental Approach?

If an 'educating' approach to CEG is accepted, then one must define the concepts which pupils might reflect upon and how these relate to environmental education. For example:

—A pupil on work experience at a car plant sees the company's Environmental Policy displayed prominently and reports on the monitoring group discussion.

—A Year 11 Geography lesson on the proposed expansion of a major city airport with local environmental consequences, employment opportunities and impact of tourism.

These examples might be considered aspects of a reflective analysis of careers from an environmental perspective. Crucially, teachers must identify the values such activities involve otherwise environmental policies may be seen, solely, as 'litter campaigns' in a different form. Schools will need to identify the trends which shape the career experience of pupils throughout their working lives. These perspectives must be built into a CEG programme in partnership with environmental education. Key markers may be:

> Hundreds of millions of people will be seeking jobs that biotech farming and automated manufacturing may make redundant. It will also occur just as multinational companies...increasingly compete for global market shares and employ every device...to achieve that aim.
>
> (Kennedy, 1993)

What is said in schools about individual career opportunity and progression?

> Clearly there exist companies and individuals (chiefly professionals providing high value added services) who benefit...and are keenly positioning themselves to gain further advantage. On the other hand, there are billions of impoverished, uneducated individuals in the developing world, and tens of millions of unskilled, non-professional workers in the developed world, whose prospects are poor and in many cases getting worse...leading to mass migrations and environmental damage from which even the 'winners' might not emerge unscathed.
>
> (Kennedy, 1993)

What schools teach of human ethics, interdependence, cooperation and competition, i.e. education, implies a deep understanding of why our world is changing. There are opportunities to discuss how other people and cultures feel about these changes, what we all have in common and what divides cultures, classes and nations. Moreover, while this process of

22

inquiry ought, if possible, to be tolerant and empathetic, it cannot be value free '...Because we are all members of world citizenry, we also need to equip ourselves with a system of ethics, a sense of fairness and a sense of proportion.' (Kennedy, 1993) The purpose of education, vocational preparation or a broad education for global citizenship, are signposts for an evaluation of the whole curriculum by schools from a careers education and guidance and environmental education standpoint.

Curriculum Design

PSE often becomes a 'slot' for all the bits of the curriculum which could not be fitted into another area. A more rational approach to curriculum design is needed, based around the fundamental values which pupils need to explore to prepare them for adult and working life. One may need to organise a curriculum which is based on a conceptual base which helps the young person, whatever its mode of delivery. The work by Buck and Inman (1993) suggests certain criteria for curriculum planning:

> Objectivity and the use of evidence to examine a range of ways of life, encouraging a critical perspective judging the quality and quantity of evidence.
> Using Concepts which enable the learner to put experience in categories, organise them and then analyse their knowledge and experience. Key concepts include:
> —choice, need, want, division of labour, rights and responsibility.
> —participatory and experiential teaching and learning styles which develop skills for independent learning including personal and interpersonal, IT, communication, decision making.

Buck and Inman identify nine key questions including:

> 'What is the nature of our rights and responsibilities in everyday life?'
> 'In what ways are the welfare of individuals and societies maintained?'
> 'On what basis do people make decisions when faced with particular choices?'
> 'How do people organise, manage and control their relationships?'
> 'What is the balance between individual freedom and the constraints necessary for cooperative living?'

These questions explore the core values of our global human culture and encourage further cross-curricular work. Reviewing core values produces a holistic curriculum design. In terms of a syllabus one could envisage a sequence of study programmes from 5 to 16 which explore these questions in a developmental way. A framework is constructed for more detailed exploration of specific issues in environmental education and in CEG. One may be freed from the tyranny of a content-driven approach and can educate pupils in the true sense of the concept.

References

Cleaton, D. (1987) *Survey of Careers Work*. London: NACGT/Newpoint.

Cleaton, D. (1993) *Careers Education and Guidance in British Schools*. London: NACGT/ICG.

Dearing, R. (1994) *Review of the National Curriculum*. London: School Curriculum and Assessment Authority.

HMI (1988) *Careers Education from 5 to 16*. London: HMSO.

Kennedy, P. (1993) *Preparing for the Twenty First Century*. London: Harper Collins.

Law, B. (1992) *Understanding Careers Work*. London: NACGT.

NCC (1990) *Careers Education and Guidance, Curriculum Guidance 6*. York: National Curriculum Council.

CITIZENSHIP AND ENVIRONMENTAL EDUCATION

Janet Edwards

Environmental issues are important to young people. Organisations with an environmental focus are among those with expanding membership. Without empowerment, participation and skills of communication, progress can be difficult for young people who wish to work for an environmentally-sound future. Citizenship education is about participation, community involvement, rights and responsibilities, democracy, the law, and the provision of services by voluntary, state or private services. Citizenship and environmental education share many common characteristics:

> Environmental education may be thought of as comprising three linked components:
> —Education **about** the environment (knowledge);
> —Education **for** the environment (values, attitudes, positive action);
> —Education **in** or **through** the environment (a resource).
>
> (NCC, 1990a)

This concept transfers well to education for citizenship. If young people are to be encouraged to take citizenship seriously, they need to be included as participative members of the community. School and the local community are stages upon which this participation can be played out. Education about participation is the knowledge or curriculum content upon which aspects of citizenship are based. Without some knowledge, discussion and decision-making are lacking a firm foundation. Education for participation involves values, attitudes and skills (of debating, negotiation and presentation). To persuade others or to consider, seriously, the views of others, demands competence in these aspects of working. It is about involvement in activities of a participative nature using the community as a resource, and people outside the school as community partners.

> The aims of education for citizenship are to:
> —establish the importance of positive participative citizenship and provide the motivation to join in;
> —help pupils to acquire and understand essential information on which to base the development of their skills, values and attitudes towards citizenship.
> Education for citizenship develops the knowledge, skills and attitudes necessary for exploring, making informed decisions about and exercising responsibilities and rights in democratic society.
>
> (NCC, 1990b)

> The Speaker's Commission on Citizenship stresses that:
> the opportunity for learning provided by the community experiences will provide an indispensable springboard to encourage students to make a voluntary contribution in later life.
>
> (HMSO, 1990)

Schools need to make clear to students what they are aiming to do as coherence in the learning process is crucial. Work which combines environmental awareness and education for citizenship has an important role. Similarly there are many links between national curriculum core and foundation subjects and the cross-curricular themes which need to be made.

> If, through the themes of environmental education and citizenship, schools are expected to re-educate society to its responsibilities they will have a key role to play by involving children from their earliest years in learning from their surroundings, using the local environment as a medium for enquiry and discovery and as a source of material for realistic activities. Pupils need to feel free to move into and out of the school building from an early age as part of the whole process of learning.
>
> (Thompson, 1993)

There are many activities which satisfy the congruent aims of education for citizenship and environmental education.

Nursery school

Children focussed on flowers in a project entitled 'The Darling Buds of May'. After selecting one flower a week to study the children then plant seeds and bulbs and watch them grow. They set up a flower shop in the nursery after visiting their local florist to see how it should be done. They reconstructed Monet's paintings of the garden at Giverny. They visit the bulb fields in Spalding before creating their own flower festival which becomes the culmination of the project. The streets around the nursery are lined with crowds of flag-waving adults and children as a parade of flower floats passes by, decorated with daffodils and tulips. Alongside these floats, parents, teachers and nursery nurses are accompanied by an energetic group of children, colourfully dressed to represent the flowers and countries of Europe.

Citizenship Concepts: Work and leisure, community.
Environment Concepts: Plants and animals.

(Walters, 1993)

Playground Project

An inner city infant school wants to improve the playground facilities to encourage more diverse and cooperative playtime activities. Teachers collect information by observation, video and questionnaires about the children's feelings and opinions on current and future provision. Meetings are held to discuss feedback and make plans. A grant and other help from *Learning from Landscapes* (Learning Through Landscapes, 1986) is obtained for changes to the playground.

Citizenship Concepts: Community, individuals and groups, use of leisure.

Environment Concepts: People and communities, cultural aspects of the environment.

(Centre for Citizenship Studies in Education, 1993)

Key Stage 2, Active Citizens

A class, in a school beside a busy road, decides to tell the local council their concerns about a subway, constructed to provide a safe way of crossing the road, but little used by the children as they find it a threatening environment. They survey opinion by questionnaire and study the problems the subway presents. In English they write prose, poetry and letters to the council complaining of dirt, darkness, graffiti, vandalism and water lying on the surface. By taking action the pupils gain in self-esteem and confidence. They focus on a local concern and do all they can to improve a situation.

Citizenship Concepts: Community, being an active citizen, public services.
Environment Concepts: People and communities, impact of transport on the environment.

(Edwards, 1993)

Secondary School Activity

A school council decides that the school environment needs to be tidier. A survey is conducted of the views of local residents and primary and secondary school pupils and teachers. The findings are used to plan an anti-litter campaign, involving picking up litter, a poster competition, talks by older pupils to assemblies of younger year groups, group work on how best to react if you witness litter being dropped.

Citizenship Concepts: Community, being an active citizen.
Environment Concepts: People and communities, buildings, management of waste and recycling.

(Centre for Citizenship Studies in Education, 1991)

Key Stages 3 and 4, Conservation

The extension of an industrial estate threatens a pond containing protected species. Local schools use the opportunity to debate the need for employment against the desirability of conservation and consider alternative solutions. They work with the council, developers and the fire brigade to re-establish the pond and all its wildlife in a new location.

Citizenship Concepts: Work, employment and leisure, public services, being an active citizen.
Environment Concepts: People and communities, endangered species

and conservation, destruction of natural habitats, impact of industrialisation and urbanisation.

(Centre for Citizenship Studies in Education, 1991)

'The Night Shelter Project'

One Upper School and the contributory Middle and Lower Schools work together. Each school conducts its own project work on 'Homes and Homelessness'. All come together on one day near the end of the summer term, at the Upper School, when they share project experience by means of an exhibition and, using waste resources provided for them, they build shelters in groups of four. They sleep out overnight in these shelters. Homelessness is a local issue. Human needs include food and shelter. Follow-up work in each school is varied and covers international, national and local projects, housing provision in the parental home, setting up home independently, rented or purchased accommodation and budgeting.

Resources: Children's Society materials (Children's Society 1991), CSV and Leaving Home Project (Hope 1989). Local Council, local churches, Police, companies provided materials for shelter building.
Citizenship Concepts: Community, being a citizen, the family, democracy, public services.
Environment Concepts: Buildings, industrialisation and waste, people and communities.

(Edwards, 1993)

'The Mineral Debate'

This is a simulation for secondary schools in which participants adopt roles of those with vested interest in whether or not further extractive industry is to be allowed around a town. The County Council's long term plan is to restrict further gravel extraction and an embargo has been placed on the allocation of any further licences to excavate. However, a major national company has discovered extensive deposits of a valuable mineral. This discovery has occurred at a time of a national recession which has badly affected the local population. Participants debate the issues and the council votes to decide whether the development application should be allowed or rejected.

Citizenship Concepts: Community, being a citizen, democracy, work, employment and leisure.
Environment Concepts: Soils, rocks and minerals, uses and management of resources, effects of extractive industries, people and communities, buildings, industrialisation and waste.

(Thompson, 1993)

28

Key Stage 3 – 'Industry in Focus'

A whole year group is involved in a week-long project. Teams of pupils engage in study of nine branches of local industry. Objectives are to increase knowledge and understanding of the economic and industrial world, local environment, local career opportunities, and political issues. The week starts with presentations from UK Atomic Energy Authority and Friends of the Earth to illustrate conflict existing at national level between industry and the environment. Each pupil visits two of the following local industries: a chemical manufacturing company, a waste disposal firm, sand and gravel extraction, water treatment, supermarket 'greening', organic and non-organic farming, testing involving animals, and recycling. The visits are reported and issues raised such as the chemical industry creates smells, increases traffic in the locality but provides employment. Sand and gravel extraction has had a devastating effect on the countryside but provides materials essential for road construction. Pupils witness the efforts of a responsible company carrying out restoration work. Each pupil will develop independence of thought, respect, tolerance and understanding of effective action to deal with matters felt to be intolerable.

Citizenship Concepts: Skills of communication and taking action, investigation, reporting, evaluating, decision-making.
Environment Concepts: Effects of extractive industries, water, plants and animals, waste.

(Thompson, 1993)

References

Centre for Citizenship Studies in Education (1991) *Citizenship Education: Broadsheet 31*. Northampton: Centre for Citizenship Studies in Education.
Centre for Citizenship Studies in Education (1993) *Citizenship in Primary Schools*. Northampton: Centre for Citizenship Studies in Education.
Children's Society (1991) *Education for Citizenship*. London: Children's Society.
Edwards, J. (1993) *Cross-curricular Theme Pack 1: Citizenship*. Cambridge: Pearson.
Hope, P. (1989) *Making the break*. London: Community Service Volunteers.
Learning Through Landscapes Trust (1986) *Play, Playtime and Playgrounds*. Southgate: Learning Through Landscapes Trust.
NCC (1990a) *Curriculum Guidance 7: Environmental Education*. York: National Curriculum Council.
NCC (1990b) *Curriculum Guidance 8: Education for Citizenship*. York: National Curriculum Council.
Speaker's Commission (1990) *Encouraging Citizenship*. London: HMSO.
Thompson, I. (1993) *Cross-curricular Theme Pack 2: Environmental Education*. Cambridge: Pearson.
Walters, T. (1993) 'Good citizens in the making', *Nursery World*, September.

INFORMATION TECHNOLOGY

Bob Hopkins

There are several examples of lessons and projects that illustrate the use of Information Technology in Environmental Education. They follow the structures first described in the National Curriculum documents for the two disciplines. *Curriculum Guidance 7: Environmental Education,* describes the coverage of the subject in terms of education about, for and in the environment (NCC, 1990). Non-statutory guidance for Information Technology describes the development of Information Technology capability across five strands which have recently been defined in two themes. (Dearing, 1994)

Dearing's recent report to the DFE emphasised that information technology is fundamental. Therefore although many of the ideas described below are equally accessible without a computer, IT can develop an increased awareness of the environment and vice versa.

Learning ABOUT the Environment

A CD–ROM called *Water* (Academic Television, 1993) contains information ranging from skiing to oil spills. A large database may be researched and individual case studies such as Dolphins, The Thames Barrier, etc, considered. Water can be studied from political, industrial, recreational and other perspectives. However, each theme is described with a mixture of video clips, sound commentaries, text and still pictures. The potential of the compact disk is only just entering schools, but as each CD is equivalent to around 500 ordinary floppy disks, they are a significant advance in accessing information.

Learning FOR the Environment

Sometimes ecological disasters happen in the vicinity of the school but more often, a sensitivity to environmental issues has to be developed in our pupils secondhand. A computer simulation called *Fishkill* can illustrate what happens. It offers the opportunity for pupils to roleplay the part of environmental scientists who are faced with an emergency situation. A quantity of dead fish in a stretch of previously unpolluted river are found. To a time-scale decided by the computer, the scientists must decide what to do. They can take water samples, examine the poisoned fish and test water upstream of the disaster. The samples are then returned to the laboratory and tests carried out to determine the cause of the deaths or the degree of pollution. The scenario can be decided or created by the teacher in advance. Pupils may have to prove a case against a factory and its industrial waste or against a farmer's excessive use of insecticide. The problems of proof, of accuracy and of diplomacy all have to be faced and overcome.

Learning IN the Environment

Datalogging is the name given to the computer's ability to record certain changes in the environment. This would normally be difficult if you wanted to monitor a riverside or bat box. The computer would be vulnerable to the elements and far from its source of power. Datalogging boxes such as 'Sense and Control', however, can be set up at the computer and then detached to be used at the work site. They monitor light levels, temperature, pH, oxygen and other environmental factors for periods up to two days. Instruments known as light gates could be located at the entrance to bird boxes and the frequency of the arrivals of bluetits to feed their young measured. School children thus have access to the rigorous observations formerly the province of the dedicated hobbyist or professional. For example the bacterial activity inside a cowpat might be enough to maintain a temperature above that of the surrounding areas. Datalogging equipment could quickly be set up to test the insulating properties of groundcover in snowy conditions. The kits need to be returned to the computer in a field centre, laboratory or classroom so as to download and examine the results. However there is the prospect of serious computing in the field.

Theme One – Communicating and Handling Information

The new A1–M1 road link provided a good opportunity for a local secondary school to abandon its timetable for some year groups and to devote the best part of a week to investigating the development of industrial estates on nearby land. Graphics programs were used to design an industrial development, word processed letters sent to obtain the information necessary to develop car parking facilities, and amenity areas incorporating access for those with special needs. Desk-top publishing programs were used to produce the plans and to persuade the local authorities and action groups that the developments should take account of the natural and working environments. IT-produced letters and plans lend authority to voicing matters of concern, advice or protest on environmental issues to politicians, newspapers and planners.

In another example children were asked to follow up their observations of the structure of the daffodil flower with a description of reproduction in plants. A carefully prepared overlay for Prompt Writer on an Overlay Keyboard ensured success in sequencing events for a group of children whose inability to produce structured writing could have made this a difficult, demotivating task. The pupils were not only successful but also highly motivated to take their work further. IT allowed them to concentrate on the ideas under review and be released from the delays involved in normal sentence construction.

There are times when the sheer quantity of information can make searching for evidence or information very difficult. Back copies of the country's newspapers are now available on CD–ROM. This makes it possible to research, for example, the contribution to the nuclear debate made by the *Times* or the *Guardian* newspapers.

Similarly, no study of the weather at Key Stages 2 or 3 is complete without some reference to past and current weather statistics. The current weather may be monitored by hand or with a datalogger. 'Is this wet for July?', 'What is meant by a miserable summer?', are both questions which require reliable statistics. A database such as 'Pinpoint' on the Acorn or 'Grass' and 'Information Workshop' on RM computers can structure these statistics in an accessible and searchable way. Many of the statistics are already available from meteorological stations around the country, although not always for use on computers. The usual database structure involves records and fields. In the case of weather data the records are likely to be the days and the fields will be the types of statistics gathered for each day. Typical fields might include date, rainfall, wind direction, temperature, wind speed and cloud cover. There is no reason why one field might not be the acidity of any rain that fell during a 24 hour period. The 'Watch' organisation have the necessary kits to make the measurements.

When learning about the environment, databases can be created or used to find information on minibeasts, butterflies, animals and so on. Once again the new CD–ROMs have a role to play and two of the first group of CDs to become available include *Creepy Crawlies* which includes details of 70 of the world's most photogenic beasts with text, sound commentary and video clips. The other is called *Mammals* and is a fairly comprehensive view of some of the world's mammals, again with video clips, stills and animal sounds.

One of the best examples of a useful database is called 'Pondlife' (Granada Television). There are three parts to this program. The first assumes a pupil has approached the computer with a jam jar containing a pond creature. The computer prompts the pupils with questions about the creature such as the number of legs, wing cases and size. From the pupil's responses the computer identifies the creature with a picture and name. The second part of the program is a database of information about any of the identified creatures which are likely to be encountered in the pond environment. The third part of the program models a pond or stream and its behaviour when populated with various life forms and when polluted in various ways (see next section).

An old, yet under-used program is called 'Branch' (Flexible Software) which facilitates the production of branching identification classifications. Pupils are shown pictures of a variety of moths and butterflies, for example, and encouraged to find questions which can be applied to all the butterflies and moths. The 'branching' system will divide the creatures neatly into two groups and teach the pupils some of the finer distinctions within the generic term 'butterfly'.

Theme Two – Investigating Models and Control using IT

Modelling is the process where the outside world is modelled in some way on a computer screen. The workings of a food chain can be replicated on a computer and the effects of pollution on the creatures concerned can be determined without any loss of life. The 'Pondlife' program can be used to model the animal and plant populations in a pond or stream. The computer first asks the user for the dimensions of the pond and the types of vegetation found there. The program goes on to ask for the creatures that might be found there and adds them to the model. When the simulation is ready the species can interact and the way the pond reaches a balance of species is shown. However, the balance can then be deliberately disturbed by, for example, pesticides, flooding and several other factors. The effects are studied in a time sequence allowing dangerous processes to be modelled safely.

Sometimes the factors that need to be manipulated are statistical and the number-crunching can be accomplished very easily by computers. A spreadsheet such as 'PSS', 'Grasshopper' or 'Excel Starting Grid' can easily be adapted to show the effects of culling elephant or seal. Too little and the environment takes over, sometimes with its own brand of cruelty or sacrifice, too many and the population falls into decline.

The laboratory is an excellent place to look for evidence about growth or animal body structure. The same instruments used in the field to monitor temperature or to keep track of the comings and goings of bats, can also be fixed up, via a 'Sense and Control' box to record the growth of plants. Such questions as, 'Is the rate of growth affected by the amount of light, minerals in the soil or the amount of water available?', can all be tracked on the computer. Similarly the hypothesis that small mammals are more vulnerable to frost and the consequences of heat loss than larger mammals, can also be tested by looking at the rates of cooling associated with the contents of large and small vessels in the laboratory.

One might also consider the use of computers to capture satellite images from space, to monitor weather fronts perhaps or study 'Landsat' images which can pinpoint changing land use in every field in a county. This is an expensive process for the school. In many cases however the expense of IT has already been met. Most schools have access to computers, to datalogging equipment and to satellite images. Those schools without access, often primary schools, could still make use of the facilities via their local authority advisory service or their local secondary schools. At the simplest levels, there can hardly be a school without its own supply of word processors, databases and spreadsheets and all can be used for environmental education.

References

Dearing, R. (1994) *Draft proposals for Information Technology*. London: School Curriculum and Assessment Authority.

NCC (1990) *Curriculum Guidance 7, Environmental Education*. York: National Curriculum Council.

Technology in the National Curriculum (1990) DFE. Attainment Target 5, Information Technology.

Address

The Watch Organisation, 22 The Green, Nettleham, Lincoln LN2 2RR.

Software

'Branch'. Flexible Software, Abingdon.

Creepy Crawlies CD–ROM. Optech Limited, Farnham.

'Excel Starting Grid'. Research Machines, Abingdon.

Fishkill. Oxfordshire County Council Computer Centre, Oxford.

'Grass'. Newman College, Birmingham.

'Grasshopper'. Newman College, Birmingham.

'Information Workshop'. Research Machines, Abingdon.

Mammals CD–ROM. Optech Limited, Farnham.

'Pinpoint'. Longman Logotron, Cambridge.

'Pondlife'. Granada Education Software, Sevenoaks.

Prompt Writer. Resource, Doncaster.

'PSS'. Cambridgeshire Software House, St Ives.

'Sense and Control'. Data Harvest, Leighton Buzzard.

Water CD–ROM. Academy Television, Leeds.

CHAPTER 3

Environmental Education and Practical Considerations

CONSERVATION ORGANISATIONS AND SCHOOLS

Sue Paice

There is no better way for children to understand environmental concepts than by becoming involved in the practical application of the principles concerned, i.e. 'learning by doing'.

Many organisations make opportunities available for pupils to participate in conservation. There are several options which are easily accessible to schools, with fruitful relationships to help children understand the importance of the links between global and local issues. Pollution, transport, overpopulation, loss of habitats and decreasing biodiversity are reflected in the school's immediate environment. Pupils can also learn to challenge the economic assumptions which usually dominate the arguments put forward about how one should care for the environment. They can come to appreciate that conflicts of interest will arise.

The global effects of environmentally-harmful activities must be understood so that pupils appreciate that the issues do not just involve Britain. Friends of the Earth and Greenpeace are campaigning organisations which collect data on international topics as diverse as the disposal of radioactive waste, overfishing in the North Sea and Brazilian mahogany production. The World Wide Fund for Nature provides schools with information on how wildlife is being affected by human activities. There are many ways in which children can be helped to do something about these issues through such organisations, who are always keen to expand their youth sections. They provide material for pupils to carry out projects, arrange events and join sponsored activities. Children can become better informed in their conversations with friends or family about how to adjust their lifestyles to be less harmful by using less water and electricity, eating fewer of the endangered species of fish, recycling materials, etc. The scenario presented by these organisations can be overwhelming so it is important to relate them to what children can do in their own sphere to contribute towards the solution. Too much bad news on its own can make children and teachers feel powerless and without hope, which is counter-productive.

On a national scale there are other organisations which can provide schools with valuable support. The Learning through Landscapes Trust is an organisation set up to help schools make better use of their grounds for conservation. They run regional conferences for teachers to give them practical advice. The Young People's Trust for the Environment and Nature Conservation is also worth contacting, as is the Council for the Protection of Rural England. The latter has commissioned a national report on how much of our countryside is being lost to development. Their 'Agenda 2000' provides valuable background for teachers whose pupils are investigating the effects of mineral extraction for example. If a school in England requires funds to set up a practical environmental project in its grounds, then English Nature has a grant scheme available, administered nationally from their Peterborough headquarters.

Locally there are many conservation organisations which schools can call upon to provide evidence of environmental situations closer to home. The Young Ornithologists' Club (the junior RSPB), the Wildlife Trusts (WATCH) and the Bat Conservation Trust (Young Batworker) all provide newsletters, posters and projects for children and help them to make a contribution to protecting the environment. WATCH, for instance, has carried out valuable ozone and water quality projects. It is important to represent these issues as topical, controversial and exciting, with plenty of graphics to catch youngsters' imaginations. These junior groups place their emphasis on practical action as opposed to textbook identification. The children who plan to specialise later in, for example, ecology or botany, can be guided onto the right track by such organisations at an early stage. Children are encouraged to gain practical knowledge via enjoyable, group activities such as a badger watch, a guided bat walk using bat detectors or a tree-planting event. As well as having fun, the children are acquiring cross-curricular skills which provide an excellent base for reaching attainment targets in Geography, Science and Technology.

Many conservation organisations help schools to see the environment as an opportunity rather than a problem. For example, taking on the management of a piece of land within the school grounds or nearby is an excellent way of putting environmental theory into practice. Some schools may feel daunted by such a challenge but should be encouraged by the example of the case study in the next section of this chapter (page 39). In Northamptonshire, the Countryside Services branch of the County Council helps many schools and community groups to set up what are known as 'pocket parks'. These are areas of land which are owned and managed by local people with access for everyone to enjoy peaceful recreation in a managed, conservation setting. Pocket parks can be havens for wildlife as well as people, and through them children can regain that contact with nature which many have lost. Thus schoolchildren learn the principles of natural succession, population dynamics and habitat creation from the local pocket park. They also learn how to explain these principles to others, which may mark the start of a long-term commitment to protecting the environment.

For those Northamptonshire schools which do not have their own parks, there is sometimes one in a nearby village or town. A strong emphasis is placed on the educational benefits when a pocket park is set up and an invitation is issued to local schools to use it as an extra classroom. Scouts and Guides can gain conservation badges there and Duke of Edinburgh Award candidates may use them for their studies. Parents and governors may become involved in weekend work parties with a common, worthwhile goal of helping the school and providing an attractive amenity for the neighbourhood.

The benefits to the pupils are, clearly, many. There is the physical one of healthy fresh air and exercise, which many children may lack because of their increasingly, sedentary lifestyle. There is the mental stimulation of satisfying their intellectual curiosity about environmental processes which are actually being promoted by the children themselves. Watching their experimental cornfield turn into a blaze of summer colour, or toads colonising their newly-created pond can be awe-inspiring for children. Because they are practically involved, their understanding is likely to be the greater.

Emotionally and socially, there are also many benefits to be gained by schools from undertaking a practical, conservation project. Although some children may be too young to understand, they too have the opportunity to respond to the spiritual dimension of life which contact with birdsong or the process of metamorphosis may engender. Teachers may benefit too. Such feelings could be brought into English if older pupils are studying, for example, Wordsworth's poetry and his views on nature.

In addition, all can benefit from a sense of pride in what has been achieved, the team spirit that has been fostered and a growing sense of responsibility for the environment, which is one foundation of a complete education. A very positive statement is being made to the outside world about what the school's values are, and everyone feels reassured that such values are being upheld.

A more tangible boost to the school's image may come in the form of an environmental award. Several conservation organisations are now making such awards available to schools, for example, Anglian Water's 'Young People's Conservation Award', Shell's 'Better Britain Campaign', The Tree Council and many of the county Wildlife Trusts.

When a school embarks upon a wildlife area or pocket park it must decide on which conservation organisations to establish a working relationship with and how to recognise and avoid pitfalls.

Two of the most important aspects of such a project are to appreciate the long-term commitment or sustainability of the scheme needed to ensure success and to gain secure tenure of the land. The pocket park should be handed on to each new generation of pupils to care for. It should be a project which, in one sense, is never complete. Another important principle is to involve the wider community, creating a valuable link with the school. It is very easy to forge ahead with an excellent project, only to have it neglected and forgotten in the summer holidays. Therefore it is vital to bring in as varied a mix of local people as possible, to share the care of the site throughout the year. This means that if the area is in the school grounds, there must be public access, which may not be acceptable to some schools. The alternative is a system of key-holders which might be complicated, hindering spontaneity.

Once a group has been set up to manage the pocket park, it is advisable to appoint a co-ordinator or leader who can liaise with the various conservation bodies and keep everyone informed of progress. The British Trust for Conservation Volunteers provides excellent resource packs and books and has field officers in most counties. The Shell 'Better Britain Campaign' produces a free guide which is available to all schools. It offers useful advice on how to get started on environmental projects. Sometimes there are county-based services, employing people who have experience in supporting projects. In Northamptonshire, which pioneered the idea of pocket parks, there is a Pocket Parks Officer who provides advice, support and grant-aid, where needed. Other counties may obtain help from environmental or tree officers or the local Wildlife Trust. The Sussex Wildlife Trust has been particularly active in promoting pocket parks, following Northamptonshire's example.

The next stage for schools is to prepare a five year management plan with a description and evaluation of the site as it is now, objectives for the future and a schedule of work for achieving those objectives. Site plans and species lists can be included. The plan may be as simple or complicated as the school desires but it does need to be an easily-understood, working document which can be passed on when the main organiser leaves the school. It is important to get the opinions of a cross-section of the school and wider community, to establish ownership of the project before the plan is written. Again Wildlife Trusts, English Nature or local authority officers may be able to help with this.

Part of being successful in any venture is anticipating challenges or difficulties and preparing for them in advance. Environmental education projects can be susceptible to vandalism. Advice on how to combat this can often be gained from the ranger at the local authority country park. Toughened perspex for interpretation panels, metal bars in gates and entrances which block motor bike access are devices which have to be considered. Finance needs to be thought through carefully, so that a project can be properly completed. The British Trust for Conservation Volunteers regularly updates a list of organisations which will provide grants to schools and conservation groups. It is wellworth schools affiliating to the Trust in order to have regular access to this and other useful information.

Another difficulty may be maintaining momentum once the novelty has worn off. One solution may be to form a network with other groups carrying out similar environmental projects, in order to exchange ideas, materials and motivation. An established group, which knows the ropes, can act as 'mentor' to a new group, awakening their own enthusiasm, as well as giving practical help to the 'novices'. Such networks are being set up in some counties by the national organisation ACRE under their 'Rural Action Scheme'.

We are fortunate in having a wealth of very active conservation organisations in this country which schools can call upon to help them promote environmental understanding and action. One must hope that future governments will make an equally strong commitment to environmental education and provide the necessary resources to enable schools to take up the challenge.

CREATING AN EDUCATION AND COMMUNITY ENVIRONMENTAL
RESOURCE

Terry Mortimer and Drisc Wardle

This is a case study of a large environmental project conducted by the staff
and pupils of Nicholas Hawksmoor Primary School with the help and
involvement of the local community. The development depended upon
cooperation between many diverse groups and organisations that came
together to create an area of considerable local importance.

The main objectives of the project were two-fold:

(a) To provide a conservation area for use by the pupils of Towcester as an
    educational resource. The town lies in an intensely cultivated farming
    area; patches of woodland and pond that remained as isolated corners of
    the landscape have mostly been cleared and drained. Access to the
    remainder is difficult as it is not within easy walking distance and is
    likely to be fenced. Landscaping of the town's open spaces has left few
    areas where the children may observe and study wildlife in its natural
    habitats.

(b) To provide a valuable leisure amenity for the local community.
    Towcester has developed rapidly in the last decade. Unfortunately
    provision of leisure amenities has not kept pace with the building of
    new houses and the town's population of some 6,000 people is left
    without a public park. The Pocket Park provides a much needed area
    for quiet relaxation.

The Pocket Park occupies land adjacent to the school field. It lies in an
area designated by Towcester Town Council for development as a riverside
walk. This is a linear park providing a walkway between the town's new
leisure centre on the edge of the town and the shopping area in the centre.
However, the land here is of a particularly marshy nature rendering it
unsuitable for traditional landscaping but most suitable for the creation of a
pond and wetland conservation area. Towcester Town Council most gener-
ously offered free use of the land to the school in recognition of its possible
use as an educational and leisure resource. A small management committee
was set up in April 1991 to coordinate the project.

A complete survey was first undertaken by the children. Aided by a gov-
ernor of the school, who is a civil engineer, they measured and 'levelled' the
area. This involved children using a variety of mathematical measuring
equipment to define the area and map its features. The children then drew
their own scale plans for its development. This work introduced the children to the concept of proportionality in a relevant and meaningful way.
Surveying and producing plan drawings taught the children complex skills

and gave them an understanding of the difficulties encountered by civil engineers and others on major building projects. It also highlighted the importance of achieving the right answer in a calculation. From the children's work a master plan was drawn up for the park's development.

Care was taken that only native Northamptonshire species were included in the planting scheme. Existing features were retained and new ones created to ensure that the maximum variety of natural environments would be available for study. These included a small lake, 125 metres of native hedgerow, a small copse or woodland area, a spring flowering and summer flowering meadow and a wetland. The management group were determined that the park should be accessible to all, including the elderly and less able. A kissing gate was installed which was specially designed and constructed to allow the passage of wheelchairs and pushchairs. Hard paths were laid to facilitate mobility by these groups and wide, angled platforms constructed to enable observation and study of the pond by people from their wheelchairs. The creation of the lake was felt to be beyond the scope of our volunteer workforce so a professional landscape contractor was employed to carry out the major construction work, thereby ensuring the success of the project. Funding for this was provided by a Pocket Park Grant, a scheme initiated by Northamptonshire County Council. These grants cover three-quarters of the cost of development; one quarter is met by Northamptonshire County Council, one by South Northants District Council, another quarter is provided by the Countryside Commission and the remaining quarter must be found by the Pocket Park Management Committee. In our case this extra quarter was supplied by the Town Council. Once the scheme has been realised advice and assistance is available from a Pocket Parks Officer to ensure correct maintenance and management.

Construction work began on site in July 1991 and quickly created the pond and paths. With the aid of Towcester Fire Brigade the pond was filled. Anglian Water had given permission for water to be drawn from a nearby brook for this purpose. The water provided was thus already rich in pond life forms and was not contaminated by the chemicals present in tap water.

Groups of children from the school, helped by members of the local community, then began the work of planting. Every child in the school grew their own wildflower plant from seed and planted them in the park. For the younger children this demonstrated the life cycle of plants, the necessity of creating the right conditions for growth and the importance of continued care to ensure the plants' survival.

In the Autumn of 1991, Year 5 and 6 children planted young trees in the area which will, in time, become a woodland. Research into tree species by the children gave information on which trees to plant and the planting distances between them. Precise and detailed measurements of the growth of these trees has continued providing children with a database of information on growth patterns for their further studies.

That same Autumn, one group of Year 5 and 6 children sowed the meadow, first dividing the land into metre squares and weighing the seed to ensure the correct quantity was used. The children then prepared the ground and sowed the seeds. This involved them in calculations of weight and area, ground measurement and ratio.

During the winter months a 'Hedgerow Planting Day' was timed to coincide with National Tree Week and was very well attended by children, parents, grandparents and other community groups. Around fifty people planted over 1,500 trees and shrubs to form a native Northamptonshire hedge around the perimeter of the park. They also set hundreds of bluebell bulbs and cowslips.

Since the completion of the major planting and landscaping the children have been responsible for a large part of the maintenance work in the park. This has included keeping the base of trees and hedges free of weeds, haymaking in the meadow and pond clearance. They have also worked to keep the area free of litter. A maintenance plan has been drawn up to ensure that the park is developed fully and safely. This provides a yearly cycle of clearance for pond and paths, hedge trimming and tree pruning. It also provides a planned timetable for mowing the meadow to ensure the continuance of a variety of species and for regular weeding and watering of the whole area.

The area is now used by all pupils in the school from nursery age to Year 6. Nursery children are currently monitoring the changing seasons and how they affect the flora and fauna. Year 3 pupils are pond dipping and recording the pond life forms present. Year 4 based their project on weather observations in the park. Year 5 is studying the growth patterns of the meadow with the use of quadrants. Year 6 regularly use the area as a stimulus for their artwork. They have recently produced close observational drawings and paintings, one of which won a first prize in the 'Britain in Bloom' competition.

All ages use the park as a practical base for their maths and science work. Because the park is situated adjacent to the school grounds, this makes regular visits easy to organise on a daily or hourly basis. With the aid of a grant from the British Trust for Conservation Volunteers, the Pocket Park Association purchased 'First Sense' measuring equipment for use by any group, school or community, working in the park. This equipment allows sensory probes to be sited in soil or water which record temperature, humidity, light, etc. The probes then feed this information directly into a computer to produce charts and graphs. Recent use of the system by Year 2 and Year 3 children enabled quite complex analysis to be undertaken by relatively young children.

The park has also been the setting for community art classes, led by the deputy headteacher. The resulting paintings were then put on display in the town's Leisure Centre. Frequent visitors to the park include elderly residents of a nearby senior citizens' residential home, and physically and mentally disadvantaged young people from a local Day Care Centre. Other local schools and youth groups including 'Beavers' and 'Brownies' have also used the park for both educational and recreational purposes. Throughout the summer it is used by families living in the locality, for walking or, often, as a site for a picnic.

Funding for projects such as these is often a major stumbling block. The group approached both local and national organisations for financial support, spreading their net widely. Though often unsuccessful, this has resulted in donations from many different sources. These have included the 'Shell Better Britain' campaign which provided a 'set up grant', Macdonalds Hamburgers who provided wildflowers, and a local charity which donated a bench seat. Approaches to local businesses resulted in many small gifts of money and equipment. The park has benefited from affiliation to the British Trust for Conservation Volunteers who have provided expert help and advice, loans of equipment and a financially advantageous insurance scheme. The Nicholas Hawksmoor Pocket Park Association is now a fully registered charity which enables it to draw on many other areas of grant aid.

Since its completion the park has been the recipient of many awards and commendations. It won the Smith and Allebone Shield, a scheme run by the Northamptonshire County Council and the Northamptonshire Wildlife Trust jointly, in recognition of the children's knowledge and understanding of conservation issues. In 1992 the school was proud to receive a gold medal in the Queen's Anniversary Trust Awards as one of over 6,000 schools from Great Britain and the Commonwealth which were entered for this award. Only six primary schools achieved this accolade. Children and staff travelled to St James' Palace to receive the award from Her Majesty the Queen and the Duke of Edinburgh. Understandably, this was a most memorable day for all concerned.

The work undertaken on the Pocket Park has made a relevant and valuable contribution across the curriculum. Working with the natural environment fosters, in the children, a deep understanding and love of their natural heritage. The knowledge of the need for continuous care and cooperation to ensure the growth of living things teaches them much that can be transferred to their attitudes in the classroom and their relationships with others. The success of the project has demonstrated to them the possibility of changing their environment for the better and the very real part that they have to play in that task, both now and throughout their lives.

CHAPTER 4

Environmental Education and Core and Foundation Subjects

ENGLISH

Ros McCulloch

> Then up I rose,
> And dragged to earth both bough and branch, with crash
> And merciless ravage: and the shady nook
> Of hazels, and the green and mossy bower,
> Deformed and sullied, patiently gave up
> Their quiet being: and unless I now
> Confound my present feelings with the past,
> Ere from the mutilated bower I turned,
> Exulting, rich beyond the wealth of kings,
> I felt a sense of pain when
> I beheld the silent trees and saw the intruding sky.

Reflecting on his action in tearing down the hazel glade, in the poem *Nutting* Wordsworth voices that aspect of the Romantic response to nature which expresses feelings of responsibility and guilt for the wilful destruction of the environment. The same note sounds in familiar works like D.H. Lawrence's *Snake* ('And I have something to expiate;/A pettiness') right through to some of the poems we present to our pupils today. The Oxford English Programme, for example, gives Key Stage 3 pupils Gwen Harwood's *Barn Owl*, a poem about a child who shoots an owl and is horrified by 'this obscene/bundle of stuff that dropped,/and dribbled through loose straw.' Finally the owl dies after the child shoots it again: 'The blank eyes shone/once into mine, and slept./I leaned my head upon my father's arm, and wept,/owl-blind in early sun/for what I had begun.'

The contribution of English to environmental awareness might start, then, by introducing pupils to poems and stories in the English canon that emphasise personal responsibility for the natural world. Many students are already committed to protecting the environment, so it is useful to use their beliefs as a starting point. However, there are additional reasons for doing so. Some students may become scientists, or go into the public domain, where they may have considerable influence. Others, though they follow paths that give them less individual power over the environment, will still have a voice that can be heard publicly, in however small a way. If, as English teachers, we can help our pupils to develop a sense of personal responsibility for the environment as well as access to a variety of ways of expressing that responsibility, we are empowering them in ways that may later influence what happens to their world.

Coming to have a view and to articulate it in a satisfying fashion is the beginning of a sense of ownership of an issue. Of all classroom subjects, English is the one where the fullest response can be made, in private and public ways. Sometimes a poem or a story read in class will impel a pupil to write their own poem or story in an exploration of personal feelings. However, such responses may not come at once. Feelings take time to be worked through before they surface in a child's consciousness. Unfortunately, today's curriculum demands can work against this reflection, but the words of Grace Nichols, commenting on her own poem *Forest*, are salutary:

> Reading back the poem I was surprised at the line, 'And we must keep Forest' because in a way, it reflects my own concern about the preservation of our forests. But I didn't set out to say this at all in my poem. I wasn't thinking of making people aware of the importance of keeping our forests. It just came out in poem. This is what makes poetry exciting for me. A poet can discover things in her own poetry. It's like going on an adventure. You don't know quite where the poem will take you because it has a living mind or spirit of its own. So one of the most important things in writing a poem is to tune in to the feelings of the poem, to listen to that still small voice in the poem, instead of forcing it to say the things you think it ought to say.

Pupils can of course be presented with environmental matters in more prosaically-rooted language work. Here too, the scope for classroom development is very wide. Questions about the environment evoke strong feelings, whether they be concerned with road-widening or rain forests. Environmental matters may seem simple, especially when they appeal so powerfully to our emotions, but the issues are more problematic. Often genuine dilemmas are involved, like the competing claims of convenience versus conservation, or utility versus aesthetics, and the best outcome is by no means always clear-cut. Change in the environment is not necessarily bad, or even where some initial damage is done, greater good may eventually result. On the other hand, although all environments change, there are those who argue that we should preserve things as they are and repair any damage. There are significantly different points of view here that need to be explored through debate and discussion.

The English classroom can usefully bring together such work. Often this is best done through cross-curricular planning, with pupils collecting evidence from work in other classroom subjects, like science or geography, and bringing the results to the English classroom. The presentation of such evidence, and the arguments that stem from it, need to be laid out in a lucid way, and for this the English classroom provides the best forum. Students can work in small groups on different aspects of a question and bring together the various strands in whole class presentation and debate. Class groupings can be arranged so as to foster the individual abilities of everyone in the class, so that each pupil, however they may have fared in more knowledge-laden subjects, feels able to make a contribution. Thus, a pupil may have difficulty with the science or the statistics of an environmental issue, but be able to give convincing rhetorical expression to their feelings. If words are their strength, they can be placed with scientific and mathematical colleagues so that the group produces a richer and fuller response than any of them could have managed alone.

Implied here is the extension of the sense of personal responsibility from the domain of private behaviour to the public. In making that move, we are asking pupils to work out their position on larger environmental issues, albeit in the safety of the classroom setting. Clearly we want our pupils, as embryonic citizens, to develop a sense of public responsibility. The step is thus an important one, and as children become more aware of environmental issues, we will want to bring to their notice some of the threats that endanger the environment. The English teacher can introduce such material through poetry and prose. Brian Patten vividly captures the sense of an invisible environmental menace in *The newcomer*, whose last stanza runs:

Through the animal kingdom
The news was spreading fast –
No beak, no claws, no feather,
No scales, no fur, no gills,
It lives in the trees and the water,
In the soil and the snow and the hills,
And it kills and it kills and it kills.

The sinister aspect of the world described in Patten's poem is that whatever 'it' is that is spoiling the world is invisible. Pupils can be asked to find examples of destructive things that are being put into the environment, from newspapers, magazines, and from what they are learning in other school subjects. Such information can be put together in the form of a collage, made up of media articles, pupils' own findings and poems and stories they have written themselves. Such contemporary material, displayed in classrooms or school corridors, will help to keep environmental issues in pupils' minds.

Alternatively, the devastated world of Patten's poem can be compared with poems that depict a less blighted nature. Grace Nichol's poem *Forest* would be an appropriate contrast. Pupils might go on to work in groups to compile a set of poems and prose on the theme of humanity's treatment of nature, which could be the subject of a dramatized presentation to the whole class, or to a class of younger pupils in the school.

Popular classroom texts like *Z for Zachariah* reinforce the theme of an environment destroyed by man, and pupils react powerfully to such texts and the discussions that they provoke. Factual material can be brought in to supplement the discussion, and the work given a practical outcome for a greater feeling of engagement with the issues. Pupils engaged in this sort of work may be writing to local MPs and newspapers, or designing and distributing leaflets to raise public awareness about an issue. For older pupils, project work can provide a focus for systematic work on an environmental issue about which they feel strongly.

Pupils being asked to respond to material like this are also entering the period of adolescence, when issues are taken with great seriousness. This is often particularly the case where there is damage or suffering to innocent creatures. Consider, for example, the strength of pupils' reaction to Brownjohn's poem *To See the Rabbit* (Brownjohn, 1983). As teachers we have a responsibility to ensure that our pupils do not take too much personal responsibility for environmental damage over which they can have no direct control. Many of the things currently being done to the environment are outside the scope of the ordinary person. They result from commercial exploitation, national and global political decisions. Very often we do not hear about these matters until things have deteriorated too far for much rescue work to be done. Adolescents can be encouraged to explore and voice their judgements and feelings on these issues, but should be protected against over-assumption of guilt.

Much of the material on environmental issues that we give our pupils is strong stuff, and we need to balance its impact by reminding them of the limits of their personal responsibility. It is one thing to regret pulling down the hawthorn glade, but quite another to feel you might have prevented the destruction of Twyford Down. Things have got more complicated since Wordsworth's time. We can, however, help our pupils to express their reactions to environmental issues in appropriate ways. These ways will, as suggested above, include letters, petitions, collages, poems, plays and stories. They will show pupils making something out of the powerful feelings evoked in them as they reflect upon the environment. The strength and the delicacy of expression that such feelings can evoke is here illustrated by a poem taken from a collection written by pupils at Beaumont Leys School in Leicester in poetry workshop sessions spread over a week in March, 1994.

A Fiery Fish
Imagine a flexible nugget of gold
Or silver, its orange glittering.
Shaped like a darting bullet
Ricocheting off the shiny walls.

With scales, layered like an onion
And an open mouth, gaping like a cave.
They say it lived in a glass, water land
And had a seven second memory span.
This beast died out with mankind
But it lives on, it is a legend.
(*Nick Brookes, Year 11*)

References

Brownjohn, A. (1983) 'To see the rabbit' in Stibbes, A. and Newbould, A (eds.) *Understanding Texts through Dramatization and Reading Aloud*. London: Ward Lock.

Eccles, D. (ed.) (1994) *Different Voices, One World*. Leicester: Beaumont Leys School.

Harwood, G. *Selected Poems*. Australia: Collins/Angus and Robertson.

Nichols, G. (1988) 'Forest' in Styles, M. and Cook, H. (eds.) *There's a Poet Behind You*. A & C Black.

O'Brien, R. *Z for Zachariah*.

Patten, B. (1985) *Gargling with Jelly*. London: Viking Kestrel.

Pinion, F.B. (ed.) (1963) *A Wordsworth Selection*. London: Macmillan.

MATHEMATICS

David Cain

Mathematics is not an exercise carried out in isolation, a kind of ill-defined limbo. One operates in an environment; the class or work room in which one sits, the sounds that are a part of the process or which intrude, the people one works with, are all part of the working environment. At the same time the mathematics in which one is engaged could well be a tool one could use, either to make an examination of the environment in which one lives or to make an impression upon it. One needs to examine both of these aspects of the relationship between mathematics and the environment.

There are schools where it is possible to enter a room where mathematics is taught and not know it until the subject is announced. There are classrooms with wooden shelves groaning under the weight of rows of identical dusty textbooks. There are corridors devoid of any kind of decoration or display. Down these corridors and into these rooms pass children who expect and are expected to engage with mathematics. They will spend a lot of their valuable learning time in an environment whose main effect is to depress and stultify. If we want children to appreciate the aesthetic beauty of mathematics then we need to create for them a working environment which is full of this beauty. There are many very attractive and stimulating posters that can be used to decorate corridors and walls. Mobiles of solid shapes can be suspended from any ceiling. Most importantly, all available wall space can be covered with children's mathematics. There can be no environment more stimulating to learning than one where both the subject and the learner are obviously held in high esteem. If the external surroundings are ugly and uncared for this will, almost certainly, be reflected in the internal responses of the child. A primary school teacher reading this may well challenge the description of a school devoid of displays to stimulate. However, let them be assured that they exist, and have been reported upon. However, there is a less obvious, yet potentially more damaging environment that can have a profound effect upon children's attitudes to mathematics. This is one created by people who clearly do not enjoy mathematics, who cannot perceive any value in it beyond its being a tool and who are quite prepared to state proudly that they are no good at it. We must do everything in our power to ensure that this mental environment is as positive as we can make it so that the children receive every encouragement to engage with mathematics. The best teachers of art clearly enjoy being artistic, teachers of English read and cherish literature. It is to be hoped that all teachers of mathematics enthuse about their subject and can be seen getting pleasure from using elegant mathematical processes.

So, having created as effective a learning environment as we can, we must use the mathematics we have learned to inform us about the wider community outside and to enable us to make some impact upon that environment.

The physical environment in which we live is an immensely complex three-dimensional structure. As we move through it the shapes of which it is made up are continually changing their size and position in relationship to us, the observer. Children can obtain great insights into aspects of space and shape, such as similarity and enlargement, by investigating what happens to the relative positions of trees, buildings and so on when they travel past them. It is possible to simulate this in the classroom by asking pupils to put five or six objects on a table in the middle of the room. They can then walk around the table and sketch the objects in their relative positions from different points of view around the table. If the table is then cleared and the pictures, together with the objects, are given to another group, then they can be asked to try to replace them on the table in their original positions. Another activity which forces children to examine carefully their surroundings is getting them to draw panoramas. On a residential visit a group of children might be taken to a good viewing point such as the summit of 'Catbells' in the Lake District, each with a compass. They could then be allocated a ten degree arc and asked to sketch what they see within this arc. When the pupils return to base they could then draw out their portion of the view on large sheets of paper, taking care to ensure that each side of their section matches with those of the neighbouring sections. The whole set of views could then be mounted around the walls of one of the workrooms. The mathematics required is not great but the pupils will certainly have studied the view from the top very carefully indeed.

Children can also examine the make-up of both natural and man-made objects and try to see how their mathematical structure relates to their efficiency and effectiveness, or not as the case may be. The links between the growth patterns of trees, the structure of a dandelion flower and the Fibonacci sequence can lead to extremely rich investigational situations. There is no need to visit the Alhambra in order to see how geometric forms and structures can be combined in breathtakingly beautiful ways. In fact, by examining the geometry of the man-made structures in which we spend our working days, the links between aesthetics, mathematics and fitness for purpose can be investigated.

Environmental problem-solving is clearly one area where there is vast scope for mathematical activity. A task such as creating a garden, a pond or a reserve for wild life will require the use of the kind of skills which should already be developing under the heading of 'Using and Applying Mathematics'. The practical skills of measuring, estimating and calculating will obviously be as much in evidence as servicing skills. However, weighing up of the priorities, the gathering of information to inform decisions, and the creation of a balance between theoretical and realistic outcomes will call for a sophistication of thought which is not too often required in the carrying out of specifically mathematical tasks. The task does not have to be on the scale of those outlined above. There are many problems that can be set to find efficient ways of packaging items for sale where more attention, from an environmental point of view, is payed to the kind of material used. An investigation into the whole area of wrapping and packaging could yield a lot of insights into the amount of waste we experience during the very ordinary activity of shopping. The concept of 'cost' can be made to take on a much greater significance if environmental considerations have to be taken into account. Encouraging children to take a closer look at their surroundings, asking them to make judgements about the efficiency of transport systems, waste disposal systems, heating systems, manufacturing systems, recycling systems will not only force them to look critically at their environment, it will also require them to develop skills in the collection, handling and display of data as well as using statistical analysis techniques.

The mathematician, like the scientist, cannot operate in a vacuum. This is not to say that there is never a time when we can do mathematics for its own sake. Wrestling with a purely theoretical piece of algebra or a combinatorial problem is an immensely rewarding activity, an opportunity to hone our intellect. However, there must also be a time when we take this intellectual capability and apply it to the solving of problems in the world in which we live. We have to make our own small contribution to the creation of a physical and mental environment where we can live at ease and use appropriate mathematical processes at will.

SCIENCE

Jeffrey Best

Despite many statements of intent and well-meant attempts to heighten the profile of science, the response in terms of numbers of students at all levels opting for science subjects has been disappointing. This peculiar, British antithesis has a considerable bearing on what follows. On the one hand, it is claimed that environmental education furnishes suitable means for introducing science in a user-friendly fashion, which ought then to assist recruitment to examinable science subjects in the later years of school and beyond. At the same time, a significant proportion of those inspired by environmental education subsequently encounter difficulty when attempting to pursue that interest in higher level courses, because of the science content. The common ground would appear to be that there is an important difference between the 'science' experienced via environmental education and the science in subject-specific disciplines, including environmental science, in further and higher education. The difference is that environmental education is highly selective in its references to science, usually from an issue-based approach, whereas formal encounters with the sciences proper, involves exposure to markedly different language, values and procedures from those underpinning other areas of the curriculum.

As has been widely acknowledged, science is intellectually demanding, requiring progressive acquisition of its distinctive mores and methods, whereas much of the so-called science in environmental education is actually partial scientism. This is not to deny its utility, but the distinction should be recognised if there are not to be misleading consequences at a later stage, to the detriment of both the student and their perception of science. Following the Toyne Report, this difficulty is no longer confined to primary and secondary curriculum development. As a provider of an undergraduate degree programme in environmental science, certain observations are tendered about the relationship between environmental education and science. Students choosing this course wish to have more than awareness. They intend to study in depth and breadth and to gain employment as practitioners. Meanwhile, there are numbers of primary and secondary pupils with aspirations to attain similar goals. Successful candidature depends largely upon their choice of examination subjects. In order to make good decisions, the question of the place of 'science' in environmental education needs to be better understood.

This 'top down' approach is of direct relevance to environmental education in the primary and secondary phases. The science in 'Environmental Science' is essentially derived from the established disciplines. However, the scope and purpose of environmental science is not only different from that of traditional science subjects, it is also in some respects contrary to their way of looking at the world. Environmental science is holistic rather than reductionist. It necessarily involves explicit scrutiny of not only natural systems, but the interactions with human systems. Moreover, from the point of view of the latter rather than the former, environmental science – as a problem-solving enterprise – seeks solutions that have more to do with the decision-making by conscious, animate beings than the outcomes of chemical or physical processes. As such, the domain embraces rather more than pure science is intended to, or is able to deal with. There are also many aspects of science that are not necessarily pertinent to the conduct of environmental science. This awkward overlap between science proper and environmental science has to be negotiated with considerable care if neither is to be misconstrued.

The contribution of science to environmental science is simultaneously conditioned by the context from which it has been derived, i.e. the paradigms of science, and the context in which it is employed, within the realm of environmental science. Much friction and misunderstanding arises from failure to acknowledge this relational consequence. From the point of view of environmental science, its demands upon science are relatively straightforward:

What is the natural world composed of?
How is it organised?
How does it behave?
How has it developed?

Conventionally, this would be delivered as study of the atmosphere, lithosphere, hydrosphere and biosphere. With explicit or implicit adoption of general systems theory, most frequently manifest in the guise of models of ecosystems and biogeochemical cycles, the systemic structure, functioning and dynamics of the natural world is thereby approached. Alongside inputs from biology, chemistry and physics, the spatial (Geography) and temporal (Earth history) dimensions are also well to the fore. There is usually consideration of the natural world at a variety of scales, from sub-cellular and sub-atomic, to global. The pure science subjects yield vital understanding about processes, in terms of transformations of energy and matter. In addition to this 'content' there is also desirable inculcation of certain fundamental attributes of science. Although the principles of chaos, catastrophe and uncertainty are now having some influence, most thought is firmly in the logical-positivist tradition, emphasising objectivity in observation, consistency in experimentation, precision in measurement and logical interpretation of results against the strictures of hypotheses, laws and theory. Complimentary practice in the use of information processing technology is *de rigueur* as an adjunct. The intention is to develop modes of behaviour akin to those of pure science, whether or not the phenomenon in question can be so described. For example, the topic of soil erosion embraces more than pure science but its comprehension, including the conspicuous 'human dimensions' is felt to be enhanced by adherence to the *modus operandi* of science proper. In order to complete the groundwork, attention then turns to the character, structure, functioning and dynamics of the human systems that impinge upon the natural world, seen as the 'environment'. Happily, the concepts of general systems theory can usefully (though not exclusively) be employed for this too, but science otherwise has little to contribute. Instead, geography, history, economics, sociology, business studies and political studies are to the forefront in this element. The crux of environmental science is then the interactions between human and natural systems. The relationships may be seen as dependence, partnership and dominance; the process of development and its impacts for both the environment and mankind. In this, the role of science is ambivalent and, in practice varies according to the outlook of the particular course team. The interface between natural and human domains is now being actively engaged by proponents of both natural and human science subjects, the way forward having been demonstrated for example, by the re-unification of human and physical geography in recent years. Hence, as the focus at last of integrated study, such issues as floodplain management, or deforestation, are being so much better illuminated.

Thereafter, environmental science proceeds to deliver its particular benefit in terms of intervention in the dynamics of the situation, attempting to manipulate processes to the advantage of the future of both natural and human systems. That is, the concern shifts from understanding to 'management'. This is the ultimate justification of the subject and the reason many wish to obtain qualifications in it today. Most courses correspondingly offer the opportunity of eventual, applied specialisation, for example land resource development, waste management, pollution control and wildlife conservation. The fundamental sciences contribute accordingly, with chemistry and physics notable in waste management and pollution control, biology in pollution control and wildlife conservation. The environmental scientist though, has to grapple with the problem of how knowledge and wisdom is to be translated into materially effective action. For this, detailed study of the frameworks, procedures and mechanisms whereby decision-making is accomplished are called for. Students need to acquire the appropriate skills so that information is reported, communicated and marketed to entrepreneurs, regulators and policy-makers. This represents an emergent area as yet imperfectly developed, but warranting contributions from management, as well as politics and media studies. Of course the recommendations to decision-makers incorporate the findings of science and those making the case need to be suitably equipped to draw sensible conclusions from them. In case it be thought that the cause of science is somehow diminished, there is desperate need both for 'boffins' who are more aware of the downstream utilisation and consequences of their products, and 'green' managers similarly informed of the upstream science of their decisions. In this respect, a sea change of attitude is in prospect, if

54

recent, key statements of policy are to be believed, that may bode well for the employment prospects of some environmental scientists. (HMSO, 1990 and 1994) Whilst it can be seen that science is integral to environmental science, it by no means constitutes all of the curriculum. Intending candidates ought to possess at least one pure science (physics or chemistry) at advanced level, (preferably, biology too), plus another subject drawn from a wider range than hitherto appreciated. This might be geography, geology, history, economics, sociology, business studies or politics.

The character of the science that is needed, has been most clearly set out in another recent government publication (Brown, 1992). It is correspondingly vital that the earlier phases of primary and secondary education stimulate interest in science. Pupils will only be adequately prepared if Science, and other subjects, are incorporated into curriculum design and delivery.

References

Brown, A. (ed.) (1990) *The U.K. Environment.* London: HMSO.
HMSO (1990) *This Common Inheritance. Britain's Environmental Strategy* Cmnd 1200. London: HMSO.
HMSO (1994) *Sustainable Development – the U.K. Strategy* Cmnd 2426. London: HMSO.
HMSO (1994) *Climate Change – the U.K. Programme* Cmnd 2427. London: HMSO.
HMSO (1994) *Biodiversity: the U.K. Action Plan* Cmnd 2428. London: HMSO.
HMSO (1994) *Sustainable Forestry: the U.K. Programme* Cmnd 2429. London: HMSO.

DESIGN AND TECHNOLOGY

Tina Jarvis

Technological development is about changing or controlling the human environment to enhance survival or improve the quality of life. Developments, such as the invention of the steam engine and car, have had far-reaching effects on both rural and urban landscapes. Even apparently, minor improvements such as the invention of the chainsaw opened the way to rapid deforestation. Although this created economic gain it often lead to ecological imbalance and loss of rain forests. In the past technological 'improvements' were usually introduced without considering their effect on society and the environment. Consequently, control over changes has been one of the strongest motivators for increased efforts to understand technology. (Layton, 1993)

It is not sufficient to teach pupils technological skills and concepts. One must also consider the possible consequences. Pupils should not feel that technological change has created complex and major environmental problems that are beyond the influence of ordinary people. Design and Technology can demonstrate that there are opportunities for taking action to improve or conserve environments. Additionally pupils are given an approach for evaluating their environment, methods for appraising different solutions and some of the skills needed for intervention.

The importance of including design of environments within National Curriculum Technology

Unfortunately the potential in design and technology for pupils to evaluate and improve environments may not be realised because of the proposed changes to the statutory Technology National Curriculum. The particular reference to environments in the first Design and Technology Curriculum (DoE, 1990) has been omitted. (NCC, 1993) In addition a reduction of attainment targets may mean that teachers concentrate on the planning and making process with little input on identifying needs and evaluating products which is recognised by Environmental Education guidance as providing the real opportunity for pupils to explore environmental issues through Design Technology. (NCC, 1990a) Consequently, teachers will need their awareness raised as to how design and technology might include worthwhile activities that will meet the advice of Environmental Education guidance and ensure that pupils do more than examine and make artifacts.

Evaluating the quality of environments and suggesting improvements

To create or improve a product or environment effectively, existing ones need to be examined in a focussed and structured way. For example, an evaluation of the local park might start by producing a detailed map and description of the physical features and facilities. Having identified the requirements of the children, their carers and other adults who use the area, the function, aesthetic quality, advantages and disadvantages of each facility can be discussed. Each suggestion can then be evaluated in terms of time, cost, materials and skills required with the intention of producing a design to improve the park. The project could be extended by including a requirement to provide facilities for visually impaired and physically disabled children. Although it is unlikely that the pupils will be able to implement many of their proposed changes, the activity will enhance their ability to look at and evaluate a familiar locality carefully.

Opportunities to create positive change

Many pupils fail to recognise that they can care and improve the environment. They also feel that intervention is beyond most adults. Plans can identify, both what is immediately possible, as well as what could be done when they become adults. Young children might evaluate and design familiar environments, e.g. their homes and school. Older pupils can study localities which are more complex and unfamiliar. However, young pupils can, successfully, examine small local businesses, and challenging opportunities for the older pupil can arise from studying the home or school.

Primary school children might look at the design of their own bedroom and discuss what features they like or dislike in order to suggest improvements such as rearranging furniture or storing toys. They might also design the ideal bedroom within a specified budget using furniture catalogues and wallpaper books. Older pupils could research and produce designs for specific needs such as a kitchen for an arthritic or wheelchair-bound person. Another project could involve pupils finding out about 'environmentally friendly' products, modern methods of heating and insulating buildings in order to improve practice in their own school or to design a home for the future.

Recently more schools have been involving their pupils in enhancing their own school grounds. The pupils have assisted in evaluating the existing facilities, producing plans for improvements, raising funds and helping with some of the installations. This raises pupils' awareness of the quality of their surroundings and that it can be enhanced. (Jarvis, 1993) Improving the school and its grounds has also frequently lead to an increased sense of belonging, more responsible behaviour and a general reduction in litter, graffiti and vandalism. (Mares and Stephenson, 1988) A series of small projects rather than one major enterprise are easier to finance, can cater for several groups of children over the years, and are more realistic about staff resources and commitment. Even where there are limited grounds or where the land is taken up by playgrounds and sports pitches, there may be opportunities to plant trees on boundaries or small woodland areas, provide hanging baskets and potted plants, or add murals and sculptures to the walls. Other successful projects have included establishing chequer-board gardens, wild flower meadows and butterfly gardens. Pupils can design additional equipment such as benches, shelters and climbing apparatus, facilities to attract birds and ponds. (Anon, no date; Cantrell, 1989; Mares and Stephenson, 1988; Young, 1990) As a natural resource changes, so ongoing monitoring and maintenance is essential, creating further opportunities for technological projects. These might include setting up a nature trail with an associated information pack, pond cleaning and creating eye-catching litter bins or posters.

Using energy and resources efficiently

The careful use of non-renewable resources should be practiced as part of technological activities. Pupils must learn to use materials economically. Efficient use and control of energy is also essential in the design and creation of mechanical and electrical products, not only for economic reasons, but also with respect to environmental considerations. When evaluating and designing such products, pupils should be encouraged to take into account the merits of using renewable energy sources and how different cultures have solved similar problems. For example, in the past some intermediate technological solutions in the Third World have been treated with disdain, whereas they are efficient solutions, well suited to the environmental resources of the locality. Examples are the use of bicycle trailers in Sri Lanka and the small-scale hydros (micro-hydro) on fast flowing streams in Peru and Zimbabwe. (Budgett and Meakin, 1993) These successes are in contrast to some 'modern' Western technologies, which were developed to suit conditions of temperate zone ecosystems and subsequently created great environmental damage when imposed on other, usually tropical, environments. (Farvar and Milton, 1973)

Balancing people's different needs

'Finding solutions to environmental problems has to take into account the fact that there are conflicting interests and different cultural perspectives.' (NCC, 1990b) These conflicts of interest may arise between different groups of people using the same location, between short-term and long-term interests, between economic progress and the need to conserve the earth's limited resources. As designing and evaluating products for specific needs is an essential part of design and technology, pupils can be helped to empathise with people of different ages, societies and cultures and recognise their varying requirements. They may also learn that it is not always possible to find an ideal solution.

Pupils planning improvements for their community can be helped to recognise that their local streets are probably intended to give efficient

58

access to people in vehicles, on bicycles and on foot. Some will be travelling through the area, whereas others will want to get to shops and other buildings. Improvements for pedestrians, such as widening the pavement, providing road humps to discourage speeding cars, increasing the cul-de-sacs and safe crossings, may not be popular with cars users. In order to cater for all users, plans may need to include a fast route with pedestrian footbridges, or mean improving public transport.

Other conflicts can be explored by designing a zoo. Pupils will have to choose between the demands of the public to see animals clearly, and the needs of the animals for a suitable environment. They may balance taking animals from their natural environment and the need to educate people to care for animals. Conservation of the ecological balance in natural environments may be weighed against improving the breeding rate of rare animals.

Other projects might include investigating the conflicts between the concrete industry needing gravel and the environmental damage created by large scale quarrying. (Jarvis, 1991) The costs and benefits of using fertiliser on farming and fishing in South American coastal areas, balancing the differences between the various interested parties involved in building a windfarm and weighing up the pros and cons of limiting deforestation in Northern India also offer scope for discussion. (Campbell et al, 1991)

Through such activities pupils may appreciate some of the factors influencing how technological development is changing their local and world environments. The approach and skills provided in design and technology should enable them to evaluate these changes and help them to begin to recognise what they might do to influence the outcomes.

References

Anon (no date) *Nature by Design: A teachers' guide to practical nature conservation.* Birmingham: Urban Wildlife Group.

Budgett-Meakin, C. (1993) 'Valuing our future' *Design and Technology Teaching,* **Vol.26**, No.1 (pp.50-52).

Campbell, B., Hogarth, S. and Millar, R. (1991) 'Pack 1 Fertilisers: Costs and Benefits', 'Pack 3 Building a Windfarm at Greyseas and Aires', and 'Deforestation' in *Teaching and Learning About the Environment*. Hatfield: Association for Science Education.

Cantrell, R. (1989) 'Why not build your own nature reserve?' *Primary Science Review,* No.11 (pp.12-13).

DoE (1990) *Technology in the National Curriculum*. London: HMSO.

Farvar, M. and Milton, J. (1973) *The Careless Technology*. London: Tom Stacey.

Jarvis, T. (1991) 'Primary technology: The value of evaluating and improving environments' *Education 3-13*, **Vol.19**, No.2 (pp.23-29).

Jarvis, T. (1993) 'Establishing and using nature areas in Birmingham and Leicestershire primary schools' *Environmental Education*, **Vol. 42**, Spring (pp.9-12).

Layton, D. (1993) *Technology's Challenge to Science Education*. Buckingham: Open University Press.

Mares, C. and Stephenson, R. (1988) *Inside: Outside*. Tidy Britain Group Schools

Research Project/Brighton Polytechnic.

NCC (1990a) *Curriculum Guidance 7: Environmental Education.* York: National Curriculum Council (p.8; (b) p.11).

NCC (1993) *Technology in the National Curriculum: Technology Programmes of Study and Attainment Targets: Recommendations of the National Curriculum Council September 1993.* York: National Curriculum Council.

Young, K. (1990) *Using School Grounds as an Educational Resource.* Winchester: Learning Through Landscapes Trust.

60

HISTORY

David Kerr

> 'Our situation is no longer shaped by environment, rather it is increasingly we who are doing the shaping and often disastrously so.' (Worster, 1989)

This change in our relationship with the world in which we live, work and play has raised the environment to the top of the modern world agenda. Talk is of a 'global village' and debate is increasingly focussed on crucial world-wide environmental questions relating to climate, patterns of technological and economic development and demographic trends.

This means disappointingly little to history teachers at present. The relationship between history and environmental education is not readily accepted nor its potential fully explored by history teachers. This is in part due to teacher prejudice but also to the relative newness of the emphasis on world-wide environmental concerns. It takes time for such concerns to filter into the curriculum. There is no long tradition of links between history and environmental education in British education as there is with other themes such as EIU and citizenship (Kerr, 1994a and 1994b). Accordingly, many history teachers have a narrow conception of environmental education. The relationship between people and their environments is deemed important but it is perceived as the responsibility of other areas of the curriculum notably geography and science. This outdated view is compounded by the lack of detail in *Curriculum Guidance 7* on potential links between history and environmental education (NCC, 1990d).

If environmental education is to be part of the concerns of school history then history teachers must be persuaded of its relevance to their teaching. They need, above all, to be convinced of the overlap in aims and purposes between history and environmental education. A useful starting-point is to raise teachers' awareness of two developments in environmental education. First, the growing interest over the past twenty years in investigating environments in the past. Second, the important role played by such historical perspectives in informing the debates about our modern environment. The environment has evolved as a significant branch of history over the last two decades, driven by developments in North America[1]. Environmental history has attracted a growing band of historians, geographers, ecologists and anthropologists interested in the historical relationship of nature to human society (see, for example, Worster, 1994; Cronon, 1992; White, 1985). They have investigated fundamental issues over time such as population expansion and exhaustion of energy resources and produced much evidence on the social and economic determinants on the changing environment. Research has shown how:

---

[1] It is claimed that the term 'environmental history' was first joined by Roderick Nash in naming a new course – American Environmental History – at the University of California in 1970.

(1) perceptions of the environment have shifted over time;
(2) all environments present choices about how they are fashioned – what choices are made and how they are portrayed is dependent on the culture of the societies involved;
(3) two trends are behind the transformation of the world's environment namely, the increase in European population and its movement across the world and the rise of capitalism and the modern industrial economy;
(4) the evolving relationship between humans and the environment is very much about prevailing values and value systems.

The reconstruction of past environments has also been marked by a strong moral concern and desire to use the findings to inform social action and decision-making about 'the kind of world we want to live in' (Demeritt, 1994). Put more simply, the desire has been to use the lessons of past decisions about the environment to inform present decisions and future choices about the planet. Thus environmental history is playing a vital role in educating people about how the decisions of past societies have shaped not only the world in which we live but our view of that world.

Awareness of such developments can help transform history teachers' perception of and approach to environmental education. Environmental education as environmental history is a much broader and more readily acceptable working definition for history teachers. It dovetails with the central aims and purposes of history teaching. History is well placed in the curriculum to make a valuable contribution to this broad view of environmental education in schools and to help pupils to develop the knowledge, understanding and skills which will enable them to participate in present and future environmental challenges.

Closer examination of the guidance for environmental education reveals the overlap with history in the knowledge, understanding, skills and attitudes to be developed and the approach to learning. The three linked components of environmental education (education about, for and in or through the environment) are present in the programmes of study in history. History offers a unique opportunity to put these components in historical context and help pupils to understand present approaches to them in the light of past experiences in other periods and cultures.

The approach to learning in the guidance document and its aims are equally familiar to history teachers. Environmental education is centred on the interpretation of evidence and the formation of rational arguments and judgements based on evidence, often concerning controversial issues. The central aim is to help pupils to develop skills and attitudes in handling evidence, in order to clarify their own values, and encourage 'informed concern for and active participation in resolving environmental problems' (NCC, 1990d). This dovetails with the aim of learning in the National Curriculum for history.

There is sufficient overlap to suggest that environmental education can be integrated as part of learning in history in numerous contexts across the key stages. The central question for teachers is how can learning in history help equip pupils with the knowledge, understanding, skills and attitudes to contribute to:

> informed and active participation...in the protection of the environment and the prudent and rational use of natural resources?
>
> (Council of the European Community, 1988)

It is not enough to assume that pursuing the History requirements will prepare pupils for their choices and responsibilities in environmental education. Successful integration requires history teachers to think through the implications of developing the broad view of environmental education as a natural part of the process of learning in history in the classroom.

History can assist best through a process of learning that helps pupils to develop a critical respect for the evidence related to environmental issues and how it is constructed and used. Above all, it includes helping pupils to understand that the relationship between human societies and the environment and the choices and responsibilities of the individual in that society to the environment is ever changing. They should also understand that choices and responsibilities about the environment are heavily influenced by social, economic, political and cultural factors. They should come to appreciate that different interpretations of the relationship between society and the environment (*Curriculum Guidance 7* is one such interpretation and the government white paper 'This Common Inheritance' (HMSO, 1990) in history lead to different questions and alternative ways of seeing things. It requires careful thought and planning in each context. There are a number of steps history teachers might take to develop this process, notably to:

(1) identify the scope that particular areas of history provide for integrating components of environmental education as part of learning in history;
(2) establish for those areas lesson intentions to help pupils to achieve the Attainment Targets in history and appreciate the interrelationship between environmental issues and social, economic, political and cultural determinants;
(3) resource the lessons and identify appropriate teacher interventions for learning;
(4) assess the outcomes in terms of pupil understanding of environmental issues in modern contexts, preferably moving from personal and local to national, international and global contexts to encourage wider understanding of issues.

This might be achieved as follows:

Context. The teacher decides that nineteenth century Britain offers the opportunity to investigate the impact of the coming of the railways on the urban environment (focussing particularly on the impact on the built environment and on living and working conditions). This context can be covered at Key Stages 2, 3 or 4 often with a local perspective.

Lesson activities. The teacher designs activities to help pupils to:
—form opinions from a variety of sources on nineteenth century Britain about the relationship between the coming of the railways and the changing urban environment and investigate how interpretations are related to the selection and use of resources;
—compare and contrast those opinions with their views about the impact of the motor vehicle on urban environments in modern Britain;
—consider their views of modern Britain within the wider context of the spread of the motor vehicle as an international and global concern.

Resources and teaching. The teacher selects a range of sources showing different interpretations of the impact of railways on the urban environment of nineteenth century Britain (these highlight the social, economic, political and cultural determinants behind the decisions about where to locate railways in particular urban environments. Such decisions produced winners and losers as evidenced by the saying 'living on the wrong side of the tracks'). The teacher then ascertains pupils' ideas about the impact of transport on the urban environment for these will affect the way pupils will approach the historical context and the evidence presented to them. The teacher turns these ideas back to pupils to enable them to review their own thinking about the impact of transport on the urban environment.

Assessment. The teacher introduces sources with different views of the impact of motor vehicles on the urban environment in modern Britain to ascertain how far pupils are able to transfer the knowledge, understanding and skills developed in the historical context to a modern one. Finally, the teacher introduces sources which highlight the impact of the motor vehicle in other urban areas across the world (for example South America, North America and the Far East) in order to encourage pupils to consider the issues in modern Britain within a wider global context.

This is not an easy process to develop. There is no guarantee that pupils will transfer their understanding of nineteenth century Britain to question the influences on the role of the motor vehicle in urban environmental change in modern Britain or will then be able to see the issues raised within a wider global context. It is vital that that transfer is encouraged if learning in history is to equip pupils with the necessary knowledge, understanding and skills to make informed choices about environmental issues. It is a learning process which encourages pupils to develop a critical analysis of society and of the changing relationship with the environment within it. Our rapidly expanding world presents major challenges in the choices and responsibilities facing future generations concerning environmental issues. The health and safety of the planet rests on those challenges being met through considered and informed debate at all levels. Environmental history warns us of the increased risk of our cumulative actions. The potential for irreversible damage to the planet is greater than at any time in the past. It makes you think but it should also make you act.

References

Cronon, W. (1992) 'A place for stories; nature, history and narrative' *Journal of American History*, 78 (pp.1342–3).

Demeritt, D. (1994) 'Ecology, objectivity and critique in writings on nature and human societies' *Journal of Historical Geography*, **Vol.20**, No.1 (pp.22–37).

DoE (1990) *This Common Inheritance*. London: HMSO.

EC (1988) Environmental Education. *Resolution of the Council and the Ministers of Education meeting within the Council*. Brussels: European Community.

Kerr, D. (1994a) (ed.) Developing Economic and Industrial Understanding in the Curriculum. London: David Fulton Publishers.

Kerr, D. (1994b) 'History and health education' in Harrison, J. and Edwards, J. (eds.) *Developing Health Education in the Curriculum*. London: David Fulton Publishers.

White, R. (1985) 'American environmental history: the development of a new historical field' *Pacific Historical Review*, 54 (pp.297–335).

Worster, D. (ed.) (1989) *The Ends of Earth: perspectives on modern environmental history*. Cambridge: Cambridge University Press.

Worster, D. (1992) *Under Western Skies: nature and history in the American West*. Oxford: Oxford University Press.

GEOGRAPHY

Patrick Bailey

Geography is an environmental study *par excellence*. Within its disciplines, maps are the most distinctive and particular means by which geographers express themselves, setting out facts and suggesting explanations. Maps of all kinds represent environmental relationships, past and present, direct and indirect. They are purposefully selective, stylised portrayals of a real world which consists of a mosaic of natural and man-made environments. Within these many and varied environments individuals and groups, cities and nations work out their most effective ways of living.

All environments are created and sustained by processes, some natural and some generated by human actions. Natural processes produce climates and vegetation climaxes. Processes generated by human actions create for example, global markets for the producers and consumers of oil, coffee, bananas, sugar, aluminium and steel among a myriad of others. They also establish different kinds of economic, social and political systems. World thematic maps in atlases may be thought of as environmental summaries, records of the stages reached in different parts of the world by these many processes working in combination to produce the conditions of human life and work.

Larger scale maps, such as the Ordnance Survey 1:50000 Landranger series, represent environments in finer detail. Such maps attempt to portray complete landscapes, everything one can see on the earth's surface, in a given area. At this scale the interactions between environmental conditions and human activities are more clearly demonstrated in the schematic picture of landscapes and townscapes one is given in the maps. It is illuminating to think of a familiar area of countryside, for example, as a kind of precipitate, in the chemical sense, of natural and human events and processes, which have worked and which continue to work together, to create what we see today. These processes include the hedged fields, prairie landscapes of modern arable farming which seems to be replacing them, and set-aside land. Industry too leaves its mark of change in the mines, quarries and power stations, new and long-established factories and areas of derelict industrial land. Villages and towns show their distinctive regional and national characteristics and link to transport and communication systems. Along with tourist areas, maps record all these events and so offer rich sources of raw materials for environmental education.

Some possibilities for developing environmental themes may be considered under the main aspects of geography to be included in the National Curriculum interpretation of the subject. This discussion complements ideas put forward in the NCC Curriculum Guidance booklets, especially Number 7 *Environmental Education*.

Geographical Skills

The skills developed through school geography courses include those of systematic observation and recording, especially in the form of maps. It also includes their interpretation, the use of photographs, various kinds of graphical representation and the use of satellite images by older pupils. These data-gathering skills are used by geographers to seek out and interpret environmental information.

Local surveys which sharpen pupils' observations of environmental quality are very important. It is easy to take familiar environments for granted, as being 'normal'. It is the business of the geographer to help children look afresh at their surroundings and encourage them to ask questions about what they see around them. For example children could be asked to consider the visual impact of a street or shopping centre and consider whether they find them attractive or capable of improvement. They might go on to note the condition of pavements, the design of street furniture, shop fronts and advertisements, the condition of paintwork, incidence of graffiti and so on. They might question whether these things have to look as they do or whether their design could be improved. This kind of enquiry can lead into discussions about who might make the improvements and the likelihood of any suggestions being accepted and carried out. Further, pupils could explore the ways in which local residents or shoppers may be able to influence those responsible for the local environment. It may be found that environmental issues in the wider world are echoed in those closely related to the local area. The effective management of traffic is a global problem yet local aspects of it are eminently mappable at the school gates. At continental or world scales some recently published atlases provide a wealth of information and ideas for environmental enquiry.

Aspects of geographical study: Places and themes

All places are environments. The first purpose of geographical education is to help the growing child acquire a bank of accurate information about 'where places are and what they are like' on a local, national and global basis. Such information is part of the essential framework within which environmental issues can be discussed constructively. In reality there are no exclusively local environmental issues or problems. All have to be examined in the widest relevant context. A debate about the expansion of roadstone quarrying in the East Midlands, for example, has to take account of the distribution of suitable rocks, often in areas of high scenic value. A locality like Charnwood Forest in Leicestershire is visually attractive and of mineral importance. The requirements of Britain's road-building programme have to be taken into account and related especially to the development of new routes. These include, for example, access roads to the Channel Tunnel and to the Humber Estuary which are growing in importance as gateways to Europe. Questions about whether road-building solves traffic congestion may also be debated.

Studies in aspects of Physical Geography

Our technological, urban civilisation is just as dependent upon conditions and processes in the natural world as were our hunter-gatherer ancestors. However our dependence is dangerously less obvious.

One useful way to study physical environments in rural and urban areas is by investigating local relief and drainage patterns and their relationship to building. All villages and towns are located and developed partly in response to relief and drainage features. In all but the flattest towns there are perceptible variations in height which can be used to trace the course of streams even though these may now run in pipes or culverts. Street names, large scale maps, interviews with residents, and old editions of O.S. maps can all help with this fascinating detective work.

Studies of people and their environments

The most influential environments within which most people live, work and are governed are human forms and systems of economic, social and political organisation of a formal or informal kind.

One example of a contemporary, all-powerful economic environment is provided by the Russian aluminium industry. The workers' life expectancy is about 47 years. Their living and working conditions are appalling. The aluminium they produce is sold at about half the price of the next-cheapest producers, Australia, Canada and Venezuela. Yet even these countries are low cost producers when compared with Britain, Germany, the United States or Spain. The Russian industry's effective environment is its country's absolute need to sell aluminium in a competitive world market to obtain foreign currency. No other circumstance, natural or economic, is more important for that country.

Environmental Studies

All aspects of geography draw together under this heading and one is reminded that human actions are inescapably related to the well-being of the natural world.

Perhaps the most powerful idea to be developed under this section is that of intervention. All aspects of human life are about intervention. Merely by eating, drinking, requiring clothes and other facilities, and producing waste even one family or village must make demands upon and modify the systems of the natural world. How much greater then is the impact on the environment of a growing megalopolis such as Mexico City, which is predicted to reach a population of 25 millions by the year 2020. The magnitude of the task of supplying water and food to so many people in one place and disposing of their waste products is staggering. It is also unprecedented in the whole history of the human race.

There are many other kinds of intervention. By substituting roofs and streets for farmland, growing towns produce an instantaneous run-off of rain into rivers exacerbating existing flood control problems. The replacement of natural vegetation with crops over most of the habitable earth has lead to a dramatic decline in biodiversity with unknown, long-term effects. Extraction and burning of fossil fuels produces toxic discharges into the atmosphere which may contribute to the 'greenhouse effect'.

There are many examples of this kind. Geography and environmental education teach us that human beings must learn to understand and moderate their interventions in the natural world if the human race is to survive. 'Spaceship Earth' is neither an inexhaustible nor an indestructible resource.

MODERN FOREIGN LANGUAGES

Wasyl Cajkler

Before the advent of the National Curriculum, modern foreign language programmes often reflected environmental concerns and the resulting contribution to students' knowledge about our environment has traditionally been quite significant. Sixth form studies would include topics such as pollution, tourism, beauty spots, the climate of the target language community. At other levels, materials reflected this interest, for example, the Collection Vécue reader about the massacre of baby seals (Lezy in eds. Buckby and Buckby, 1985).

Environmental awareness-raising was not statutory and it could be argued that 'positive' outcomes were incidental rather than pre-planned. Nevertheless, modern language courses have long included a focus on environmental issues.

National Curriculum expectations and approaches

Modern foreign language studies are expected to contribute in a planned way to the development of knowledge, understanding and skills in this important domain. With regard to acquisition of knowledge about the environment (NCC, 1990), Areas of Experience of the Modern Foreign Languages Programmes of Study include Everyday Activities (*Area A*), The World Around Us (*Area C*), The World of Education, Training and Work (*Area D*), The International World (*Area F*), all of which afford opportunities for study of environment-related content. NCC guidance (1990) stresses all aspects of the curriculum contribute to environmental education. MFL programmes offer opportunities for study of climate patterns in other countries, of ways of life, of people and of their communities.

Textbooks already offer opportunities for exposure to environment-related content. McNab and Barrabé (1992a) present a unit on animals with students reading about the possible extinction of elephants and preparing posters that promote elephant welfare and protection. In the same work, appreciation of the earth's riches is also promoted (McNab and Barrabé, 1992b) and comparisons of daily life across the globe are facilitated. Mary Glasgow Publications' *French~for the National Curriculum* includes a students' book and cassette devoted to the environment. (Hurren, 1993) Other recently produced course books provide similar opportunities and for post–16 study, this trend is maintained, for example, with the subscription series *Thématique/Thematisch* (Mary Glasgow). There is no shortage of material. In addition, opportunities for 'real' experience also exist, for example, the log of oceanographer Jean-Louis Etienne available on Minitel via Campus 2000 (*Language World,* March 1994).

The challenge to teachers of modern languages

National Curriculum proposals (DES, 1990) focussed on the contribution that modern languages could make by suggesting that learners would be able to talk and write about issues of interest and concern to themselves, including environment. Cross-curricular activity could be organised by languages departments themselves, through inter-departmental projects or through the teaching of other subjects in the target language. The proposals suggested that the second would be the most appropriate response. (DES, 1990).

With the final proposals, the relationship to other areas of the curriculum was re-emphasised. Students of modern foreign languages should be offered the chance to explore links with other subjects and to develop knowledge, understanding and skills related to environmental education (DES, 1991). Working with other subject departments is strongly encouraged, in single lessons, in a series of lessons, on joint projects or in Key Stage 4 short courses. Examples of such cooperation have been reported, but pressures on teachers often leave little time for such creative planning. Unwillingness to engage in cross-disciplinary projects (Gayford, 1993) may account for some of the lack of development. Nevertheless, this may become more readily achievable, with post-Dearing revisions, as links with other subjects at Key Stage 4 become more accessible in the slimmer core curriculum.

Modern languages lessons have the potential to develop knowledge, understanding and skills related to cross-curricular dimensions and themes. *Modern Foreign Languages Non-Statutory Guidance* (NCC, 1992) offers pollution as a topic for study in Key Stage 4 with focus on daily routines, health and fitness, industry, advertising, international organisation, designing and marketing all featuring as contexts for the study of the topic. However, the section on differentiation in the *Guidance* offers a Year 10 target group an extremely challenging example of a unit of work, a worthy aim, but one must examine how fruitful and realizable this is in practice. The scenario described seems more attainable in Year 12 than in Year 10. While reading and listening tasks are possible at this level, it is hard to envisage many 14 to 15 year old learners being able to use another language in detailed discussion of dangers to the environment unless more time is devoted to the study of the foreign language. There is the danger that students who struggle to express views, for lack of language, may suffer demotivation and develop negative attitudes not only to the language but also to the subject matter. Teaching environmental education through the foundation subject may limit opportunities for understanding where students' subject achievement levels vary greatly.

One must consider how successfully environmental issues can be covered in language lessons that are conducted predominantly in the target language. With the Dearing Review, first language study in Key Stages 3 and 4 can be restricted to 315 hours of instruction, with some learners restricted to 262 hours. In this time, it is no easy task to promote language proficiency and integrate cross-curricular themes such that learners speak and write about them with purpose and success. In addition, second language courses receive less time, possibly as little as 180 hours. Given the demands for success at GCSE, there may be a temptation to pay lip-service to the environment, possibly to resort to token lessons on an environmental problem. However, since the prescribed areas of experience focus on the world around us and the international world, environmental education is integral to the Programme of Study. The issue cannot be passed over.

In the Programmes of Study, emphasis is placed on the development of knowledge, understanding and skills. These can be gained through collaborative, problem-solving and data-gathering approaches in real or simulated cross-cultural contexts. However, students should also be helped to acquire attitudes and values needed to protect the environment (NCC, 1990) and be encouraged to participate in the resolution of environmental problems. Many courses seem to involve a focus on the problems associated with the environment. The dangers of a series of gloom-laden topic-based units of work have been explored (Gayford, 1993). Rather than focussing on the problems of the environment, perhaps modern language teachers should seek to explore the environment as seen by speakers from other cultures in order to 'develop an appreciation of the natural, built, social and cultural environments' (Gayford, 1993) of the communities speaking the target language. This appreciation would represent a considerable contribution to general education, whatever the students' level of achievement in the foreign language.

Approaches and strategies

The development of positive attitudes to the learning of languages has long been a concern in secondary schools. An obvious strategy is the educational visit abroad, planned jointly with a history or geography department. While useful, this does not affect all students equally. MFL teachers have striven to foster a positive appreciation of the value of a foreign language to the comprehensive development of all learners. This aspiration should inform approaches as teachers seek to promote respect for the beliefs of other peoples, greater cross-cultural understanding and concern for the global environment.

The *Non-Statutory Guidance* (1992) lists topics in MFL that focus on environment in Key Stage 3 and Key Stage 4: on forms of travel and their effects on the environment, energy sources used in the home, waste disposal, noise pollution, products used in the home. Within the latter, scope exists for the exchange of information with partner schools in the target language community. Schools could exchange survey information on products used in the home, on recycling practice, on examples of successful attempts at

72

environmental protection in the home. Such activities could assist not only the development of attitudes but also of skills, such as gathering and evaluating information, entering it on a database and working cooperatively with others.

The atmosphere of the department also contributes much to a developing appreciation of the richness of our environment and the need to work at its enhancement. Attractive, regularly maintained displays, respect for resources used in the classroom, respect for differing points of view, promotional posters in the target language, commitment to the creation of a pleasant working environment (Thompson, 1993). These qualities, when regularly evident in classroom life, carry messages about the value of students' own surroundings. Such respect for the immediate environment promotes attitudes that help students address issues and establish a growing sense of environmental responsibility which can be shared with speakers of other languages.

References

Association for Language Learning (1994) *Language World*, March.

DES/WO (1990) *Modern Foreign Languages for ages 11 to 16*. London: HMSO (p.48, paras.8–10).

DES/WO (1991) *Modern Foreign Languages in the National Curriculum*. London: HMSO.

Gayford, C. (1993) 'Environmental Education' (Chapter 8) in Verma, G.K. and Pumfrey, P.D. (eds.) *Cross Curricular Contexts: Themes and Dimensions in Secondary Schools, Volume 2*. London: Falmer Press.

Hurren, C. (1992) *Environment in MGP French for the National Curriculum*. London: Mary Glasgow Publications.

Lezy, D. (1985) 'Le massacre des bébés phoques' in Buckby, M. and Buckby, N.M. (eds.) *Collection Vécue Pack*. London: Nelson.

Mary Glasgow Publications (1993) *Thématique/Thematisch*. Mary Glasgow Publications.

McNab, R. and Barrabé, F. (1992a) *Avantage 1*. London: Heinemann Educational (b) pp.94–101).

NCC (1990) *Curriculum Guidance 7 Environmental Education*. York: National Curriculum Council.

NCC (1992) *Modern Foreign Languages Non-Statutory Guidance*. York: National Curriculum Council.

Thompson, I. (1993) *Environmental Education*. Cambridge: Pearson Publishing.

Verma, G.K. and Pumfrey, P.D. (eds.) (1993) *Cross Curricular Contexts: Themes and Dimensions in Secondary Schools, Volume 2*. London: Falmer Press.

ART

Martin Wenham

Following the identification of Environmental Education as a cross-curricular theme, the more detailed guidance given on its development (NCC, 1990a; CCW, 1992a) recognized the potential contribution of art to this area of teaching and learning. As the Welsh Advisory Paper points out, 'Environmental Education is frequently at its most powerful when it is approached through the arts and humanities. Providing pupils with opportunities to learn in and from the environment can involve 'sensing'...and shaping materials...to create and express impressions and feelings'. (CCW, 1992b)

This and similar statements are welcome in that they recognize art as 'the missing component in environmental education' (Adams and Ward, 1982b) and acknowledge the major role which art education can play in developing the knowledge, understanding, awareness and action needed to improve the relationships between citizens of the future and their environment. But as they stand, such statements, even when supported by detailed case studies and suggestions for teachers (see, for example, NCC 1990b), are insufficient. If teachers are consistently to create effective teaching-learning experiences for their pupils and themselves, a deeper understanding is needed, both of art and its relationship to the environment.

Here, as elsewhere, the key to understanding the contribution which art has to make to the curriculum as a whole is a changed perception of art itself as an activity. Art can be viewed as a synthesis between two opposing tendencies, which may appear to be in opposition but are in fact complementary. The first is characterized by an individualistic approach, with an emphasis on creativity, originality and expression. The second tendency is to emphasize the social nature of art, which is seen as an activity rooted in tradition, but centred on investigation, exploration and communication. In Europe and America during the present century there has been a strong tendency to value the individualistic approach over the social, so that in education the potential of art as a means of investigating, experimenting, discovering and communicating has been underestimated and under-exploited.

As the Statutory Orders for Art in the National Curriculum imply, however, there is a need to redress the balance, to recognize that developing knowledge, understanding and the ability to communicate through investigation is as important a part of art education as the expression of feelings, ideas and themes through creative activity. (DES, 1992; Adams and Ward, 1982c)

Investigation and Communication

All learning is carried out by way of exploration and dialogue with the world around us, whether it be with people, books, toys, machines, objects of art, music or the wider environment. Art as an activity has its foundation in visual exploration and investigation. This is clearly recognized in the current National Curriculum, where the Attainment Targets and Programme of Studies for art are based on the development of visual perception (AT1) and visual literacy (AT2). Visual perception is the ability to observe; to see with understanding, both the real world and what is remembered or imagined. Visual perception, together with the skills of analysing and recording what is observed, underlies the more complex skills of visual literacy, which is the ability to 'get information from what we see...to understand at a conscious level the visual language used within a particular culture' (Zimmer and Zimmer, 1978).

Visual perception and visual literacy can be developed only by investigating for ourselves what is around us, and responding to what our environment (including works of art) has to communicate. As the examples provided in the National Curriculum show, visual exploration of the wider environment is an essential part of this process. If such investigation, analysis and recording are linked to environmental education, they can provide the basis of visual experience from which not only art work, but information, opinions, values and action can develop (Adams and Ward, 1982a).

When designing and making, the artist or craftsperson carries on what is in effect an investigative dialogue with materials and the developing workpiece, whether it be painting, drawing, sculpture, pottery, textiles, woodwork or whatever. In the course of this dialogue, new possibilities arise and are exploited: the process is one of constant experiment and criticism, modification, acceptance and rejection. 'Every good work of art...communicates the sense that something in it has been newly tried. The artist is always in training' (Scharf, 1962). This is no less true of pupils in school as it is of established professional artists, and when the work undertaken has the environment as its focus and subject-matter the interchange becomes a three-cornered one, with the artist exploring both the environment and the developing work simultaneously, using each to explore the properties and possibilities of the other.

This being so, it is to be regretted that the detailed advice in *Curriculum Guidance 7* fails to identify visual investigation through art as a major means of gathering knowledge and information. Three linked components of environmental education are identified: education about the environment (knowledge); education for the environment (values, attitudes, positive action) and education in and through the environment (a resource). (NCC, 1990c) The role of art in the second and third components is clearly charted; but in spite of the development work of the Art and the Built Environment Project (Adams and Ward, 1982a), it has no place in the first.

The guidance is that sufficient knowledge about the environment can be developed through scientific, technological and geographical investigations. This narrow approach to finding out about the environment makes sense only if the beauty or ugliness of our environment is of no concern. If we care about the environment and wish to improve it, an essential part of what we have to learn about it concerns its visual quality, both what it is, positive and negative, and what it might become.

There is extensive literature on the visual quality of the environment, much of which is concerned directly with helping the reader to develop the visual perception and literacy needed to view it critically, understand what it has to offer and how it might be conserved or improved. Much of this has been addressed to architects and planners, but some of the older work, which has achieved classic status, is a very valuable introduction and source of ideas for teachers interested in exploring environmental education through art (or vice versa). Particularly useful and accessible are Fairbrother (1974) on the landscape and environment as a whole, and Cullen (1971) on the urban 'townscape'. The ideas of Cullen and others, applied in the context of secondary and sixth form art courses, form the basis of the Art and the Built Environment Project (Adams and Ward, 1982a), which provides a very useful resource for teachers, using the processes of visual exploration and critical appraisal to develop a synthesis between art and environmental education. Extending the same approach to include the primary sector and the wider environment is the most obvious way to develop the use of art work as a means of communicating the findings of investigations and ideas for improvement and conservation.

Creation and Expression

The emphasis which has been placed here on the more social aspects of art as a means of investigation and communication should not be read as devaluing its role in developing individual creativity and expression. In a balanced concept of art, the two are seen as working together, not in conflict. A useful viewpoint in thinking about the creative-expressive dimension of art in relation to environmental education is one which contrasts objects of art and works of art (Wollheim, 1980). Put very simply, the idea is that the object of art, the actual physical object which the artist or craftsperson produces, is distinct from the work of art, which is seen as the response of the spectator to the object; the meaning and emotion which persons create for themselves as a result of seeing and interacting with the object. The significance of this idea in the educational context is that it emphasizes the importance of what is learned, felt and experienced by the artist through the process of making the object, and by the spectator through the process of interacting with it visually. The point is made that art gives us the opportunity to evoke intuitive, emotional responses, as well as rational ones, through visual rather than verbal language.

One of the simplest and most direct ways to evoke such responses is by way of symbols. Examples with which children may already be familiar are those used by conservation groups: the giant panda of the World Wildlife Fund and the avocet of the RSPB, for example. Others which have been used to represent threatened wildlife in Britain include the badger, hedgehog and wild orchid. Similar images, particularly if simplified from a representational into a graphic form (as the panda and avocet have been), can be used to represent environmental and conservation issues locally, provided that those to whom the message is addressed will immediately 'read' the symbol and recognize its significance. Powerful messages, particularly messages of protest, can be conveyed by violently contrasting images, which may combine the representational with the symbolic. One famous example coupled a photograph of a Palladian mansion and its park with a tyre track, brutally superimposed in black. The proposed motorway across the park was never built.

The imaginative-creative approach is also useful when pupils are investigating and expressing a concern for environments such as tropical rain forest or high mountain wilderness, which they cannot experience at first hand. Ideas and images to evoke mood and personal response to such environments and their plight can often be derived as much from the fantasy of Henri Rousseau as from the clarity of Ansel Adams' photographs, but whatever sources are used, effective work will both depend on and develop pupils' visual perception and literacy.

As a final example, art made in and from the environment offers an approach to personal response and creativity which seems to be very much under-exploited at present. This related to the 'Land Art' of the 1960s and '70s, but is much smaller in scale and usually more decorative and ephemeral. The outstanding exponent of this art form is Andy Goldsworthy (Goldsworthy, 1990), who uses material from an environment to create an object of art within it, which may last only for a few hours, but which is recorded by photography. Using Goldsworthy's photographs as stimuli, pupils and teachers with no previous experience, working in school grounds, gardens and the landscape, have consistently produced remarkable and beautiful results. Work of this kind provides what is in some ways a paradigm of the relationship between art and environmental education. A feeling is generated of contact with and empathy for the earth, which can help both pupils and teachers to the realization that mankind is not above the environment, nor in control of it, but is a part of it and all the changes which it undergoes.

Neither the problems nor the solutions are new. Nearly half a century ago, Alan Jarvis wrote:

> Because day in, day out, we see so much, and because so much of what we see is familiar, our sense of awareness of our environment...becomes blunted. We see, as we live, by habit...The result of the indifference of the vast majority of us to our visual environment is the increasing degradation of our surroundings...Herein lies

the vicious circle whereby each generation is forced, in self-protection, to shut its eyes to the environment...The circle will be broken only by increasing our own and our children's awareness of our surroundings and, having learned to see them, by being determined to change them.

(Jarvis, 1948)

The problem is still with us, but so is the vision to confront and solve it. In doing this, the partnership between art and environmental education has a central, not merely a peripheral role.

References

Adams, E. and Ward, C. (1982a) *Art and the Built Environment*. London: Longmans ((b) p.22; (c) pp.30-33).

CCW (1992a) *Environmental education (Advisory Paper 17)*. Cardiff: Curriculum Council for Wales ((b) p.18).

Cullen, G. (1971) *The concise townscape*. London: Butterworth Architecture.

DES (1992) *Art in the National Curriculum*. London: HMSO.

Fairbrother, N. (1974) *The Nature of Landscape Design*. London: Architectural Press.

Goldsworthy, A. (1990) *Andy Goldsworthy*. London: Viking Penguin.

Jarvis, A. (1948) *The Things we see: indoors and out*. Harmondsworth: Penguin (pp.3–5).

NCC (1990a) *Curriculum Guidance 7: Environmental Education*. York: National Curriculum Council ((b) pp.20-25; (c) p.7).

Scharf, A. (1962) 'Geoffrey Ireland: poet with a camera' in *Penrose Annual for 1962*. London: Lund Humphries (pp.29-40).

Wollheim, R. (1980) *Art and its objects (Second edition)*. Cambridge: Cambridge University Press.

Zimmer, A. and F. (1978) *Visual literacy in communication*. Amersham: Hulton Educational (pp.15 and 21).

PHYSICAL EDUCATION

Angela Wortley

The National Curriculum Council's publications, *Curriculum Guidance 7* (NCC, 1990) and *Physical education in the National Curriculum* (NCC, 1992) virtually exclude Physical Education as a possible contributor to environmental education. One would suggest that this results from a lack of understanding from environmentalists about the nature of physical education (P.E.) which extends beyond the purely physical. The publication of *Curriculum Guidance 7* predated the statutory orders for P.E. which include Outdoor and Adventurous Activities, and this may partly account for the scant references to it in the document. The narrow interpretation of the aims of P.E. in the statutory guidelines compounds the situation. Careful reading of both documents reveals the possibilities for environmental education. These possibilities can be more explicitly stated to show where P.E. can:

> Provide opportunities to acquire the knowledge, values, attitudes, commitment and skills needed to protect and improve the environment. Encourage pupils to examine and interpret the environment from a variety of perspectives -- physical...political...technological...aesthetic, ethical and spiritual.
>
> (Curriculum Guidance 7, 1990)

In order for P.E. to succeed in making a valuable contribution to environmental education, each department needs to seriously examine its curriculum, question its current practice and the attention it gives to environmental issues. Teachers need to reappraise their own attitudes towards recreational use of all environments and decide to what extent these match the school policy statement on the environment. An environmentally friendly approach by the department would force teachers to adopt teaching strategies that include environmental awareness and work towards developing, in students, a positive attitude towards creative use of the environment for sport and recreation. An audit for environmental education in a local school revealed that the P.E. department thought they bore no responsibility towards it. (Bishop, 1992)

A large percentage of school P.E. takes place out of doors in spaces that science and geography might exploit for environmental education. Outdoor exercise is an important factor in making physical activity enjoyable for many participants. A sense of awe, wonder, freedom and the pure enjoyment of open spaces are enshrined within the aims of outdoor and adventure education. The growth in demand for recreation spaces of a diverse nature in the countryside has resulted in the formulation of guidelines, planning laws, parliamentary Acts and strategic plans to give all users access. Glyptis (1991) suggests that the large number of people wanting countryside recreation must work together to more strongly advocate flexible schemes, which are environmentally protective and positive, otherwise:

they could lose out to increasingly – and unnecessarily – powerful and articulate protectionists.

(Glyptis, 1991)

Physical education teachers have the opportunity and responsibility to help students develop positive attitudes to the environment as consumers so as to ensure that they maintain and increase access to the countryside and urban open spaces for recreation and sport.

Education through the Environment

Effective school policies start from an audit of the whole school environment. This should include the indoor and outdoor spaces for P.E.; changing, storage, display and access areas. Often these are neglected in schools and present an image that does not value the quality of the environment for physical activity. It would be comparatively easy to improve the general appearance of, and provide adequate facilities to maintain the cleanliness of the area, e.g. mud scrapers and adequate paved entrances to playing fields. Well-maintained notice and information boards would further enhance the environment and could include information about environmental issues as they relate to sport in particular. Physical educationalists have to provide far more than a physical experience if they are to succeed in developing active lifestyles in students. The whole experience is important and creating clean and welcoming venues which challenge the traditional sweaty, masculine image is a major factor in the success of modern facilities. Schools need to treat this issue seriously.

Physical education can contribute to playground development projects through all key stages. Work in this area could easily and profitably move beyond the traditional design and technology boundaries. Students could become involved in resolving the tensions between creative and destructive use of the environment for recreational and sporting use. They might consider the conflicting demands and agree solutions that go some way towards satisfying all users.

Education about the Environment

Sperle and Wilken (1991) state that:

> compared to other sources of pollution, such as industry, sport certainly contributes relatively little to the harmful effects on the environment. However this does not relieve it of the obligation to minimise the burdens it places on nature and the environment as far as possible.

Personal experience leads the author to suggest that few sportspeople seriously engage in the debate concerning the impact of recreational and sporting pursuits on the environment. It is generally accepted that there is a need for substantial growth in facilities to meet present and future demands.

The environmental impact of providing these facilities, many of which are intrusive and require large tracts of scarce land, is at present inadequately debated. It is important that users of facilities need to develop a critical awareness of the issues pertaining to increased provision. This could result in more appreciation of the view of others and raise the importance of environmental considerations in sporting developments to the benefit of all. Within normal lessons, teachers could interweave a dimension that raises the issue of students as consumers of leisure and considers how all activities affect the environment to some degree. The following are some of the questions that could be posed to raise awareness:

Can/should playing fields be landscaped into the surrounding area?
How far do sports buildings intrude into the environment and what needs to be done to improve their appearance?
Are such changes affordable?
What factors determine the type of structure, its site and the materials used?
What are the concerns about floodlighting facilities?
Why do golf course developments attract so many objections?
Can noisy leisure pursuits like motor racing and shooting be accommodated in an acceptable way?
How can national sporting festivals be made more environmentally friendly (e.g. London Marathon, Wimbledon, British Grand Prix)?
What level of change to the existing environment is permissible for recreational and sporting use?
Are new activities like Ambush! (a combat game) creative or destructive uses of the environment?
Do the advantages of taking part in water-based sports outweigh the disadvantages caused by their impact on water courses?

Physical Education staff could build up resource packs to provide interesting case studies for inclusion in Personal and Social Education modules or environmental education events. The development of sports facilities within urban areas provides frequent, local examples of the tensions between participants and residents and would provide excellent starting points to consider the questions posed above. It is important that teachers go further than 'explore the potential for physical activities within the immediate environment' (NCC, 1992) and consider both the impact of these activities on the environment and others in the community.

Education in the Environment

In Finland the 'Move on behalf of Nature' National Campaign is trying to emphasise the importance of physical activity in nature as a context for intellectual, ethical and aesthetic growth (Vuolle, 1991). Telana (1991) reports that in Nordic countries the natural environment has been found to be an important motivating factor for physical activity. In Britain the Outdoor Education Movement has emphasised the impact of outdoor and adventurous activities on the development of the individual across the social, psychological, moral, aesthetic, intellectual and physical domains. Humberstone (1993) provides a critique of the diminution of Outdoor Education within National Curriculum documentation. In order for teachers to go some way towards accessing the potential benefits in personal growth for their students, they need to again, go beyond the guidelines in the Programmes of Study for Outdoor and Adventurous Activities which concentrate on safety matters. Not until (and only in) Key Stage 3 is any appreciation of or respect for the environment, mentioned. This utilitarian approach to the outdoors, sidelines the importance of introducing students to the aesthetic and emotional experiences that the natural environment offers. The sense of exhilaration and humility which so many experience are not mentioned. Importantly, it is from this perspective that students will be better able to appreciate the delicate balance between use and abuse of the environment. P.E. teachers, alone, can approach all their outdoor education from this standpoint, ensuring that all students have the opportunity to experience natural and remote environments that are likely to arouse aesthetic and emotional responses. Crucially, teachers should encourage students to reflect on their outdoor experiences from this perspective. This is more likely to affect the attitudes and future actions of students.

Conclusion

There is a strong case for increased environmental education within P.E. The aim of all departments should be to promote environmentally friendly behaviour within the framework of practising sport and related activities. The starting point will be to critically examine their current physical working conditions and departmental statements concerning the environment.

References

Bishop, V. (1992) Environmental education: A Study of a Cross-curricular Theme and its Implementation in an Upper School in Leicestershire. Unpublished M.Ed. Thesis, University of Leicester.
Glyptis, S. (1991) *Countryside Recreation*. London: Longman/ILAM Leisure Management.
Humberstone, B. (1993) 'Equality, Physical Education and Outdoor Education – Ideological Struggles and Transformative Structures?' in Evans, J. (ed.) *Education and Physical Education*. London: Falmer Press.
NCC (1990) *Curriculum Guidance 7: Environmental Education*. York: National Curriculum Council.
NCC (1992) *Physical Education in the National Curriculum*. York: National Curriculum Council.

82

Sperle, N. and Wilken, T. (1991) 'The Potential for Environmental Protection in University Sport' in *Conference Proceedings FISU/CESU Conference, Sheffield, 1991.*

Vuolle, P. (1991) 'Physical Activity in Nature' in *Conference Proceedings FISU/CESU Conference, Sheffield, 1991.*

MUSIC

Linda Hargreaves

Music is a powerful artistic medium through which pupils can be encouraged:

—to express their ideas and views about the environment;
—to examine and interpret the environment from an aesthetic perspective;
—to become aware of and curious about the environment and to participate actively in resolving environmental problems.

(NCC, 1990a)

Music is also a consumer of rare timbers, a source of pollution, and a weapon of psychological warfare. It can be shown how and why music can and should contribute to environmental education.

There are at least three reasons why music should make this contribution. The first is music's communicative power. In the West, popular performers such as Bob Geldof and Band-Aid, Sting and Paul Simon have made millions of people aware of the effects of environmental issues in Africa and South America by means of recorded music. Briceno and Pitt (1988) however, include descriptions of projects, run typically by young people, in rural India, Africa and South America which show the importance of live music, dance, drama and poetry in informing rural communities of environmental threats. Tobayiwa (1988), deploring the intrusion of European educational methods in Zimbabwe, recalls the value of learning through songs:

We learnt the alphabet in song, learnt how to spell in song. We even learnt to speak English in song. Our teacher knew how to reach us.

(Tobayiwa, 1988)

Secondly, because music is not a static medium it can illustrate environmental processes which change over time such as:

—cycles – the water cycle and acid rain;
—ecosystems – the disequilibrium caused by deforestation;
—layering – atmospheric layers and climatic change.

The following quotation might inspire a composition in three movements or a musical collage about climatic change:

The earth's climate changes. It is vastly different now from what it was 100 million years ago when dinosaurs dominated the planet and tropical plants grew at high latitudes; it is different from what it was even 18,000 years ago when ice-sheets covered much more of the northern hemisphere. In the future it will surely continue to evolve....In part the evolution will be driven by natural causes...But future climatic change...will probably have another comparably important source as well: human activities.

(Schneider, 1990)

Almost uniquely, music can model the nature of change, however slight or sudden. Key Stage 3 and 4 students could experiment with ways to represent qualitative change, e.g. metamorphosis, mutation, and pollution, by a change of instruments, rhythm or tonality. Quantitative change as in growth, or increased pollution, or decreased resources could be represented musically by an increase or decrease in one musical element such as loudness, tempo, or pitch. As students discuss and try out ways to model these changes, they will be developing their understanding of environmental processes and musical elements. *Music in the National Curriculum* (DES, 1992) in each Key Stage refers to composing music in response to a wide range of stimuli, including 'everyday sounds', 'sounds from the environment' (Key Stage 1) and 'compose a piece on an environmental theme' is a Key Stage 3 example.

A third reason for music to be part of environmental education is for the sake of music itself. In spite of the wealth of environmentally inspired music in the Western orchestral repertoire (by e.g. Debussy, Delius, Elgar, Mendelssohn, etc.) music was nearly left out of *Curriculum Guidance 7*. It finally appears in a drawing of a bit of paper tacked on to the last page before Appendix 1. In view of this add-on status accorded music in the minds of the working party, music coordinators must actively promote music as an expressive medium and participate in cross-curricular teams. Primary music coordinators will find Wheway and Thomson's (1993) *Explore music through geography* invaluable for work with non-specialist colleagues. It is full of simple and clear composition tasks and listening suggestions with titles such as *Sounds of town and country*; *Timespan*; *Gravel pit*, a composition project about the effects of mineral extraction on the local environment; *Recycled paper, Rainforest*, a Key Stage 2 rhythm layering activity; and more. *Explore music through science* in the same series is also very helpful. For Key Stage 3, Ellis's (1987) *Out of bounds*, is a very good source of materials and musical projects on environmental issues such as pollution and nuclear energy. These projects will enrich the status of music in the curriculum if music staff work in teams with other subject specialists. Royle et al., (1993) describe in detail a Year 8 collaborative music, geography and Welsh project based on the Braer oil-tanker disaster off the Shetland Isles. This project had environmental, economic and industrial understanding and citizenship education components.

Curriculum Guidance 7 (NCC, 1990) gives several examples of environmental projects in which music could play a part. For example, the Key Stage 2 project involving links with Nigeria could have included music in the artistic exchanges. In *The Nature Trail* (NCC, 1990b) for Key Stage 1, the children were blindfolded to help them focus on listening to sounds such as their footsteps, and on feeling textures such as tree barks. After the trail, instead of the visually mediated follow-up activities suggested, they could have continued to work with sound, and, as the *Non-Statutory Guidance for Music in the National Curriculum for Wales*, suggests:

—selected and tape-recorded, or sampled, the sounds;
—selected sound sources e.g. body sounds, instruments, sticks and pebbles, to
 imitate the sounds heard;
—made up new words to a known tune to recall the walk;
—incorporated the sounds into a class sound picture.

(CCW, 1992)

They could have modified the popular *Ant Trail* activity, for example (see Leicestershire Arts, 1992). The trail is drawn on a large sheet of paper and the regions where certain sounds (e.g. footsteps on different surfaces; road noises) were heard are shown. This forms the score. The children decide, in small groups perhaps, how to make the various sounds encountered including the sound of the children themselves. One group then makes the 'children' sound as someone slowly points with a finger the way along the trail. As the finger enters each region, each group makes appropriate sounds with or instead of the 'children's group'. Many variations can be made to this basic idea and it can be adapted for any environmental setting, e.g. city centre, seashore, school building.

The NCC document does not develop the idea but the examples imply a progression from simple description and recording of environmental states and events at Key Stage 1 through the identification of environmental changes, to determining potential problems and proposing solutions to them by Key Stages 3 and 4. The awareness of the conflict between environmental and economic issues and the need to find compromises becomes more prominent in the later key stages. Students will find many ways to express such conflict through music.

Music ABOUT the environment

The examples given up to this point have been mostly music about the environment and it is easy to find examples of Western music which apparently represent aspects of the environment. Walker (1990), however, traces the history of this controversial idea back to Plato and warns strongly against the temptation to apply this Western musical belief to the music of other cultures. Key Stage 3 and 4 students could have a present day version of the nineteenth century debate about representation in music, and find 'pure' and representational musical extracts to support their arguments.

Music FOR the environment

Music's capability to express and arouse emotion can be used to the full in environmental education in composition and listening work. Groups should be encouraged to discuss the issues involved and express their views in the music. They could prepare variations to suggest the attitudes of, e.g. road-builders, car users, local people and environmentalists to a new motorway (and see *Gravel pit*, above). The roles of songs and actions in getting clear messages across could be explored.

Music IN and THROUGH the environment

Both in and through the environment, music is a culprit. It pollutes the environment in supermarkets and city shopping malls. People have filed court cases against their music-loving semi-detached neighbours, where musical taste, boredom thresholds and preferred volume levels were incompatible. In schools, antagonism between musicians and other staff about sound levels is not unknown. There is scope for research, role-play, debate or real life negotiation here where the domains of citizenship and environmental education overlap. As for music through the environment, older students could find out more about the sources of raw materials for instruments and debate the use of rare materials, such as ivory, ebony, rosewood and mahogany. This may culminate in an improvisation played entirely on recyclable instruments made from paper, cans and, with care, glass.

References

Briceno, S. and Pitt, D. (eds.) (1988) *New ideas in Environmental Education*. London: Croom Helm.

CCW (1992) *Music in the National Curriculum: Non-statutory Guidance for Teachers*. Cardiff: Curriculum Council for Wales.

Department of Education and Science (1992) *Music in the National Curriculum*. London: HMSO.

Ellis, P. (1987) *Out of bounds: music projects across the curriculum*. Oxford: Oxford University Press.

Glover, J. and Ward, S. (eds.) (1993) *Teaching music in the primary school*. London: Cassell.

Leicestershire Arts (1992) *Music in the primary school: materials for the general classroom teacher*. Leicestershire Arts, Leicestershire County Council.

NCC (1990a) *Curriculum Guidance 7: Environmental Education*. York: National Curriculum Council (p.3; (b) p.20).

Royle, E., Bowden, A. and Jephcote, M. (1993) 'EIU and Music' *Economic Awareness*, September (pp.23–27).

Schneider, S. (1990) 'The science of climate modelling and a perspective on the global warming debate' in Leggett, J. (ed.) *Global Warming: The Greenpeace Report*. Oxford: Oxford University Press (p.44).

Tobayiwa, C. (1988) 'The Midnight Classroom in Zimbabwe' in Briceno, S. and Pitt, D. (eds.) *New Ideas in Environmental Education*. London: Croom Helm (p.139).

Walker, R (1990) *Musical beliefs: psychoacoustic, mythical and educational perspectives*. London: Teachers' College Press.

Wheway, D. and Thomson, S. (1993) *Explore music through geography*. Oxford: Oxford University Press.

RELIGIOUS EDUCATION

Mark Lofthouse

'And God saw everything that he had made, and, behold it was very good' (Genesis, 1.31). So ends the first part of the Genesis narrative, the description of the completion of the heavens and earth – how God created all living things and planted a garden eastward in Eden, a garden destined to be ruined when man and woman ate from the tree of knowledge. The magisterial severity of the biblical prose and its poetic fire still has the power to strike awe into an older generation. Who, for example, can easily forget the picture of Adam and Eve walking in the garden during 'the cool of the day' shortly before all hell is let loose? (Genesis, 3.8) While such scenes currently continue to resonate in a collective cultural memory, it is doubtful whether they will do so for very much longer. Religious echoes are fast fading. Biblical prose has little impact on a generation of children whose collective ignorance in all areas of belief would, in earlier times, had detonated a national scandal. (McKic, 1993)

Voices from the new right do in fact define the present state of religious education in Britain as a national scandal. (Burn and Hart, 1988) While this assertion may, or may not, be true, the generation of a state of moral panic fuels the development of a 'back to basics' agenda. (Cohen, 1972) An examination of this agenda is important because I would argue that it seriously threatens good teaching in the areas of both religious and environmental education. Moral panics invariably breed scapegoats. Currently the blame for falling standards, both intellectual and behavioural, is pinned upon teachers, who are castigated for failing to do what everyone else in society has half forgotten, namely, behaving by codes underpinned by Christian ethics. Such an analysis precipitates a rush to put old wine into new bottles. The positive attributes of sound, Bible-based religious knowledge are revisited by those who find virtue only in the past. (Jeal, 1994) While such attitudes seriously set back the cause of intelligent religious education, they threaten environmental education with extinction. The latter is viewed as new-fangled fiddle-faddle, because environmental education is not deemed to be a proper subject. In this context the 1993 Dearing Review of the National Curriculum is ominously silent concerning cross-curricular themes. (Dearing, 1993) The Dearing mission of 'slimming down' a bloated curriculum, begins to appear as a cover for a return to curriculum orthodoxy based on subjects.

The intellectual incoherence of the 'back to basics' movement should not lull teachers into underestimating the potential threat. It has often been remarked that ideology is proof against reason. The potentially destructive force embodied in 'back to basics' can be demonstrated by working through a concise case study.

Let us pursue the rationale for biblical teaching in terms of linking the

Genesis story within an environmental topic, tackling the theme of creation. Practical, professional issues confront the teacher at every turn. Firstly, regardless of the age range envisaged, what is the status of the biblical narrative? In a multicultural society, the Bible is now one sacred text among many. Secondly, if the Genesis story is to be treated as poetic fable or sustained allegory, how does this stand against a backdrop of Bible literalism, currently thriving and spreading far beyond its breeding grounds in the southern states of America? Evangelical fundamentalists do, however, have a point to make. If, in re-working the Genesis narrative for younger children, the text assumes the qualities and attributes of a 'fairy story', what is to stop children thinking of the Bible as one long fairy story? The problems increase with older children. Linking scientific and allegorical explanations together makes the latter appear, at best, whimsical, and at worst, stupid. Perhaps the best contemporary commentary on the perils of peddling Bible stories without very careful consideration is offered by a ten year old girl, whose hand shot up after listening to the sentence which begins this chapter. 'Please, sir,' she said, 'how do we know God is a he?'

This pupil's perceptive response deserves attention. Significantly the student, wise beyond her years, is interacting with the text. This in itself is worthy of commendation rather than repression. Indeed, interaction is welcomed by teachers, most of whom are all too accustomed to the apathetic boredom displayed by the majority of students when confronted by 'traditional' R.E. The idea that pupils will suddenly and reverentially change their learning and behaviour modes because the Bible has been involved, is sadly mistaken. The naivety of this perception is matched only by the notion that hell fire and damnation can be revived in the interests of curbing crime. (Kay, 1994) The notion of religion as a means of achieving social control began to disintegrate during the Victorian period. (Inglis, 1963; McLeod, 1974; Yeo, 1976) It is now, in this particular respect, a spent force. Wrenched from an informal and supportive cultural context the Bible, like other cultural icons (including, for example, the works of Shakespeare) has no unique ability to speak to a generation which has lost the keys to both respect and understanding.

So, what is to be done? Tossed about in the confusions and uncertainties of a post-Christian (Gilbert, 1980), decidedly secularized society (Chadwick, 1975), there is a strong temptation for R.E. teachers to succumb to despair. Like John Bunyan, it is difficult not to hear all too loudly and insistently the mocking voices of Doubt and Despair. As pollution rises and the ozone layer dwindles, environmentalists may well share similar doubts and anguish. I wish to argue that in the face of pervasive anxiety, considered action provides the best form of therapy. Therefore in concluding this chapter I have three objectives:

—to set out the defining qualities of Religious Education;
—to demonstrate where R.E. and Environmental Education should over-

lap and, on occasions, integrate;

—to offer information as to where relevant sources can be obtained.

The Defining Qualities of Religious Education

The pace of secularization in Britain has meant that for some time there has been utter confusion regarding what constitutes religious education. While this debate is properly ongoing, teachers may find it helpful to keep in mind the following points. Religious education is:

- ultimately and intimately concerned with spiritual issues and questions;
- it confronts students with the possibility of a God (or some kind of divine presence) active in the world and not to be relegated to the side lines of history;
- it is essentially concerned with exploring beliefs and values and how these determine decisions and behaviour.

Such a definite and challenging framework tends to make teachers feel uncomfortable. It certainly helps to explain one of the unacknowledged rituals of school life, namely an agitated headteacher behaving like Coleridge's Ancient Mariner, 'stopping one in three' by the staff room door when an R.E. lesson requires to be covered. Many teachers shrink from the task for a variety of reasons. Quite apart from feelings of mutinous despair at losing a precious 'free' lesson, experienced professionals are unsure of R.E., often in terms of both knowledge and skills. Because they are unsure in these areas, they have genuine anxieties regarding their own personal integrity in teaching what they, and others, find confusing. (Patten, 1994) Acknowledging the possibility of a God or a divine presence in the world is an intensely personal matter. Personal belief, or lack of it, does not however preclude teachers from entering into a serious consideration of values and behaviours. It is precisely at this point that colleagues working across R.E. and environmental education need to make common cause.

Religious Education and Environmental Education: A Common Agenda?

Before being abruptly consigned to the dustbin of history (Baker, 1993), the National Curriculum Council undertook pioneering work in areas of cross-curricular themes and dimensions. NCC *Curriculum Guidance 7, Environmental Education*, has been extensively referred to in this book and I have no wish to be unnecessarily repetitive. However, in setting out appropriate and relevant Skills and Attitudes for students to acquire in studying Environmental Education, the NCC authors are providing significant action points to which R.E. specialists should pay attention. *Curriculum Guidance 7* stresses the need to promote within students:

appreciation of, and care and concern for, the environment and for other living
things;

independence of thought on environmental issues;

a respect for evidence and rational argument;

tolerance and open-mindedness.

(NCC, 1990a)

These points are worth quoting in full because they unerringly replicate
skills and dispositions identified at national and local levels in the R.E.
field. (Wilson, 1993 and Northants LEA, 1987) Here the common cause is
made explicit. Collectively these skills, attitudes and dispositions provide
the means for cooperation between and across the two curriculum areas, not
least in terms of pupil profiling and records of achievement. Giving priority
to skills and attitudes is one way of additionally underscoring the importance in R.E. and environmental education of active learning. Doing things
with children is, in most cases, preferable to preaching at them. For this reason I am hesitant to be too prescriptive in terms of defining curriculum
areas and content. In terms of my own planning and teaching, however, I
have found a single sentence from the *General Thanksgiving* to be a useful
organizer. 'We bless you for our 'Creation', 'Preservation' and all the
'Blessings' of this life.' (ASB, 1980) Whether ascribed to a divine inspira-
tion or not, these three headings provide key starting points for integrated
R.E. and environmental education across the age range.

Access to Resources

When considering the current interest in returning to formal teaching, one
is tempted to suspect, pessimistically, that the problem of resources is exert-
ing an undue influence. How much quicker, safer and cheaper, for example,
to tackle 'Creation' by reading the biblical narrative (*Education*, 1994) as
opposed to involving children in creating a wild life garden, planting trees,
bulbs, plants, or enabling them, in some way, to create and care for their
immediate environment. At primary school level one book which forges a
path adroitly through the resources maze and offers imaginative approaches
to creation stories and activities is, *Religious Education Across the Curriculum*. (Rankin et al., 1991) Activities advocated in this book tie in well with
advice on creating, or following a Nature Trail in *Curriculum Guidance 7*.
(NCC, 1990b) In moving across to the 'Preservation' theme, Ian Thompson's teacher pack, *Environmental Education* is essential. (Thompson,
1993) By setting up a series of challenging workshops and exercises,
Thompson poses profound theological as well as environmental questions.
Importantly he avoids the kind of stereotypical responses which can ruin
good practice in this area: for example, God made, good; Man made, bad. In
confronting stereotypes and political correctness (Rees, 1994) teachers
have the disturbing prospect of going beyond what are too often con-
veniently, and misleadingly, labelled 'third world' problems.

Third world problems are all too often our problems and money – its management and exchange is often the linking theme. Many secondary schools operating under schemes of devolved financial management are handling budgets running into millions of pounds. Increasingly they are managed and assessed by criteria applied to a medium sized business. In this context, the ethics of financial management and wealth creation are certainly as relevant as the depletion of the rain forest. (Smith and Warr, 1994; Davies, 1994) How the issues might be linked is explored in excellent teaching packs and materials from Oxfam, Traidcraft and Shared Interest. (Oxfam, Traidcraft and Shared Interest)

In conclusion let us examine 'Blessings', the counting of which is greatly undervalued in terms of sustaining our individual and institutional mental health. If the word itself strikes you as quaintly old fashioned, substitute 'celebrations'. OFSTED has recently observed that many schools fail to celebrate enough and that negative teacher expectations significantly contribute to pupil underachievement. (OFSTED, 1993 and 1994) This lengthy contemporary thesis was some time ago elegantly summarized by Henry James, who wrote in 1879, 'Small children have many more perceptions than they have terms to translate them: their vision is at any moment richer, their apprehension even stronger than their...producible vocabulary.' (James, 1897) Perhaps, therefore, our greatest sin is consistently to underestimate our children, in particular to underestimate their resilience, their talents and their potential to save our world. Many children I work with have an intuitive grasp of what was written by a nun in the seventeenth century, whose words sum up the spirit and point of this chapter:

> With all its sham, drudgery and broken dreams it is still a beautiful world. Be careful. Strive to be happy.
>
> (Desiderata, 1692)

References

ASB (1980) *The Alternative Service Book; A General Thanksgiving*. London: SPCK, Cambridge University Press (p.104).

Baker, K. (1993) *The Turbulent Years: My Life in Politics*. London: Faber and Faber.

Burn, J. and Hart, C. (1988) *The Crisis in Religious Education*. The Educational Research Trust.

Butler, C. (1994) 'R.E. in Law and Spirit' *The Tablet*, No. 69, 19 February (pp.212–213).

Chadwick, O. (1975) *The Secularization of the European Mind in the Nineteenth Century*. Cambridge: Cambridge University Press.

Cohen, S. (1972) *Folk Devils and Moral Panics*. London: MacGibbon and Kee.

Davies, P. (1994) *The Mind of God*. London: Penguin.

Dearing, R. (1993) *The National Curriculum and its Assessment (Final Report)*. London: School Curriculum and Assessment Authority.

Education (1994) 'Devastating Certainties' *Education*, 15 April (p.294).

Gilbert, A.D. (1980) *The Making of Post-Christian Britain: A History of the Secularization of Modern Society*. London: Longman.

92

Inglis, K.S. (1963) *Churches and the Working Classes in Victorian England*. London: Routledge and Kegan Paul.

James, H. (1897) *What Masie Knew*. Preface to the New York edition.

Jeal, T. (1994) *Livingstone*. London: Pimlico.

Kay, W. (1994) 'Crime and Nourishment' *Times Educational Supplement*, 25 February (p.8).

McKie, D. (1993) 'On Those Rare Occasions when God and Mammon Meet' *The Guardian*, 15 November (p.20).

McLeod, H. (1974) *Class and Religion in the Late Victorian City*. London: Croom Helm.

NCC (1990a) *Curriculum Guidance 7, Environmental Education*. York: National Curriculum Council (p.6; (b) p.20).

Northamptonshire Local Education Authority (1987) *School Assembly and Worship: Towards a Policy for Good Practice*. Northamptonshire LEA: Standing Advisory Council for Religious Education (pp.1–27).

OFSTED (1994) *Review of the National Curriculum and Assessment: Implications for School Inspections*. London: HMSO.

OFSTED (1993) *The Handbook for the Inspection of Schools and Frameworks for Inspection*. London: HMSO.

Patten, J. (1994) 'Religion's New Place in the Curriculum' *The Tablet*, No. 69, 19 February (pp.207–208).

Rankin, J., Brown, A. and Hayward, M. (1991) *Religious Education Across the Curriculum: Topics for the Primary School*. London: Longman.

Rees, N. (1994) *The Politically Correct Phrasebook*. London: Bloomsbury.

Smith, P.M. and Warr, K. (eds.) (1994) *Global Environmental Issues*. London: Hodder and Stoughton.

Thompson, I. (1993) *Cross-Curricular Theme Pack 2, Environmental Education*. Cambridge: Pearson Publishing.

Wilson, K. (1993) Moral and Spiritual Education. National Commission on Education, Briefing Paper No.19, September (pp.1–4).

Yeo, S. (1976) *Religion and Voluntary Organisations in Crisis*. London: Croom Helm.

Addresses
OXFAM, 274 Banbury Road, Oxford OX2 7DZ.
Shared Interest, 31 Mosley Street, Newcastle-upon-Tyne NE11 1BR.
Traidcraft Exchange, Kingsway, Gateshead, Tyne and Wear, NE11 0WE.

CHAPTER 5

Environmental Education and other relationships

ENVIRONMENTAL ISSUES IN THE UK AND INTERNATIONAL TREATIES

Issy Cole-Hamilton

In 1991 the government made a major commitment to children and young people throughout the UK. Just over two years after the General Assembly of the United Nations formally adopted the *UN Convention on the Rights of the Child* it was ratified by the UK Government. In doing so it committed itself to working towards full implementation of the provisions and standards set by the Convention, and to promoting the civil, political, economic, social and cultural rights of all the UK's thirteen million children and young people. The Convention describes these rights, and associated Government duties in forty separate Articles. Amongst many other responsibilities, is the duty to ensure every child and young person, up to the age of eighteen years 'such protection and care as is necessary for his or her well-being...and, to this end...take all appropriate legislative and administrative measures'. (Article 3.2) There is also the duty to ensure that all children and young people have the opportunity to 'enjoy the highest attainable standard of health'. (Articles 2 and 24.1) Physical surroundings have a major impact on the health and development of children. They are affected by housing policy, access to public facilities and services, town and country planning, transport policies and environmental pollution. Despite the fact that the UK is party to a number of international agreements and treaties relating to the environment, many children and young people still face environmental hazards.

In the UK primary responsibility for policy relating to the physical environment lies with the Department of the Environment (DoE), although the Department of Transport also has a crucial role. Current policy stems from the World Health Organisation (WHO) 'Health for All' policy and targets adopted by the thirty-two Member States of the European Region of the WHO in 1984. In 1989, twenty-nine European countries, including the UK, adopted the 'European Charter on Environment and Health' as part of their strategy to fulfil the 'Health for All' targets for environmental policy. A new framework for UK policy, related to the environment, was developed and published in 1990 in the White Paper 'This Common Inheritance'. It covered a wide range of issues and promised regular, statistical updating of the information it contained. (Brown, 1992)

In 1992 the Earth Summit took place in Brazil and resulted in commitment from the government to implement 'Agenda 21' by adopting 'national sustainability strategies', increasing the participation of children and young people in matters of environmental policy, and producing periodic national implementation reports. The UK Government is committed to producing a report covering progress towards sustainable development in the UK, the first sections of which were published in January 1994. The DoE also publishes an annual report which describes recent and future policy development and includes its future expenditure plans. (Annual Report, 1993) The Department of Transport publishes a similar report. (Department of Transport, 1993) The UK is also party to the 'Montreal Protocol', an international agreement on the phasing out of the chemicals involved in ozone layer depletion.

The most prevalent environmental threat to the life, health and development of children and young people in the UK today is accidental injury. Accidents are the largest single cause of death for children aged one to fourteen and resulted in about two million attending accident and emergency departments annually. (Department of Transport, 1992; CAPT, 1989) For children from one to four years old, accidents are most likely to occur in their homes. For older children and younger people the biggest threat is road traffic. Accidents happen amongst all groups of children and young people but are most common among those from low income families and deprived areas. (Levene, 1992; Sharples, 1990; CAPP, 1993) Twice as many boys as girls die from accidents. (Jackson, 1992; CSU, 1992)

Government strategy concentrates on educating the public to adopt safer behaviours but there is little discussion of legislation and policy to remove the causes of accidents or to ensure that parents and carers have sufficient resources to make their homes and neighbourhoods safer. (Pankhurst, 1992) Education about accident prevention can only be effective if it meets the needs and circumstances of different groups of people and is supported by effective, legally enforceable, controls over the design, planning and construction of the environment in which the child is growing up.

A further major threat to children's health and development is poor housing. Local authority environmental health officers and trading standards officers are often under-resourced, hampering their ability to monitor existing laws and regulations. At the same time, housing policy over the 1980's had lead to a massive reduction in good quality, low-cost housing.

Feeling safe and secure in the local environment is crucial to health and development but is not the only important factor. Development also involves widening experiences and increasing independence. The needs of of children and young people must, therefore, be an important consideration in the planning and development of the local environment and transport systems. Facilities, designed with children in mind, provide enormous potential for enhancing their physical, mental and social development. Conversely, children whose opportunities for play, social interaction and independence are restricted or denied, can suffer developmentally. At present most facilities and services in the UK, used by the general public, are designed by adults for adults, with little or no consideration given to the needs of children. Outdoor play facilities in both urban and rural areas are often badly maintained and vandalised. (BTG, 1991) In urban and rural areas, there are fewer and fewer open spaces in which children and young people can entertain themselves safely. For those with disabilities and learning difficulties the problems are even greater. Combinations of the design features, which restrict access to public places for many children, can cause particular difficulties for those with disabilities. (DA, 1991)

Transport and the potential for independent mobility are also important in the development of children and young people. However, evidence shows that children's freedom of movement is becoming increasingly restricted, predominantly by road traffic. Transport policy is developed with very little regard for its impact on children's independence. (Hillman, 1990) Apart from the effect of restricted mobility on mental development, children do less physical activity than previously with potentially harmful effects on their long term health.

Environmental pollution is a major threat to health. In the UK today one urgent problem is the close link between increased asthma and other respiratory disease in children and air pollution from road traffic. Other problems include the continuing presence of pesticide residues and heavy metals, such as lead, in food and water, and land surface pollution. Monitoring of environmental pollution and its effects is inadequate. Most information collected is based on adult exposure and potential effects. It does not take into account the particular vulnerability of children. Despite promises by the government at the World Summit in 1992 to strictly enforce the 'precautionary principle' and the 'polluter pays', there is recent evidence that the government is failing to take these promises seriously.

Children and young people in the UK take environmental matters seriously. There is considerable interest in local neighbourhood issues, especially conservation and safety, and much distress caused by the apparent lack of long term policies to protect the wider environment. Article 12 of the *UN Convention* states that children and young people have the right to express their opinions on matters which affect them and have those views taken seriously. Despite widespread interest there are very few opportunities for active involvement in the planning and development of local

96

communities. Support for environmental education is not consistent.

The *Convention* also describes the right to education which develops respect for the natural environment (Article 29(e)). Education and participation are interlinked and lack of environmental education is a concern for children and young people. (BCC, 1992) However, a survey carried out in 1991, among a random sample of schools, found that environmental education had a low priority. (RSPB, 1992)

Examples exist of where Article 12, the right to express a view, and Article 29(e), the right to environmental education, are being put into practice. In one, a 'Safe School' project in a primary school in Hillhead in Glasgow, the work lead to an understanding of why strict rules applied to dangerous places, e.g. stairways. The project involved children, parents, governors, teachers, the PTA, the LEA and local health board. (CAPT, 1993; Roberts, 1993) 'Learning Through Landscapes', a scheme for involving children and young people in the design and planning of their school environment, is another important initiative.

Greater involvement means consulting with children and young people from all sectors of the community at the beginning, and throughout, service planning and development. It should be implicit in all local environment statements, strategies and policies. Consultation, like equal opportunities, is everyone's responsibility.

References

BCC (1992) Birmingham Young People's Conference. Birmingham City Council. 21 November.

Brown, A. (1992) *The UK environment. Department of the Environment.* London: HMSO.

BTG (1991) *Danger – Children at Play.* Birmingham Townswomen's Guild.

CAPP (1993) *Epidemiology of Childhood Accidents – first report of April 1993.* Belfast: Child Accident Prevention Project.

CAPT (1992) *Basic Principles of Child Accident Prevention.* London: Child Accident Prevention Trust.

CAPT (1993) *Safe schools are no accident.* London: Child Accident Prevention Trust.

CSU (1990) *Home and Leisure Accident Research: 1990 Data.* London: Consumer Safety Unit, Department of Trade and Industry.

DA (1992) *A Charter of Rights.* Belfast: Disability Action, April.

Department of Health (1992) *The Health of the Nation.* London: HMSO.

Department of the Environment (1993) *Annual Report 1993 – the Government's expenditure plans for 1993–94 to 1995–96.* London: HMSO.

Department of Transport (1992) *Road accidents Great Britain 1991.* London: HMSO.

Department of Transport (1993) *The Government's expenditure plans for Transport 1993–94, 1995–96.* London: HMSO.

Hillman, M. et al. (1990) *One false move...A study of children's independent mobility.* London: Policy Studies Institute.

HMSO (1990) *This Common Inheritance.* Cmnd 1200. London: HMSO.

Jackson, H. (1992) 'Accidents in schools' *Child Safety Review,* December (p.4).

Learning Through Landscapes. Winchester: Learning Through Landscapes Trust.

Levene, S. (1992) 'Preventing accidental injuries to children' *Paediatric Nursing*, **Vol.4,** No.9 (pp.12–14).

Pankhurst, L. (1992) 'The Health of the Nation' *Child Safety Review*, December (p.5).

Roberts, H. (1993) 'Safe schools are no accident' *Primary Health Care*, **Vol.3**, No.4 (pp.18-20).

RSPB (1992) *Environmental Education in England – Report of Survey*. Sandy, Beds.: The Royal Society for the Protection of Birds.

Sharples, P. et al. (1990) 'Causes of fatal childhood accidents involving injury in a Northern region, 1979–86' *British Medical Journal*, 301 (pp.1193–7).

WHO (1990) *Environment and Health: the European charter and commentary*. Copenhagen: World Health Organisation Regional Publications, European Series No.35.

98

MORAL AND VALUES EDUCATION

Mike Cross

Educational aims are often couched in broad terms. The aims of environmental education are no exception. According to the National Curriculum Council's *Curriculum Guidance 7, Environmental Education*, 'The long-term aims of environmental education are to improve management of the environment and promote satisfactory solutions to environmental issues.' The broadness of these aims, improving the management of the environment and promoting satisfactory solutions to environmental issues, has important links with teaching about moral values.

Acid rain, the Green Belt issue, the gassing of badgers (examples from *Curriculum Guidance 7*) are all issues which raise questions about the treatment of the environment. Amongst these questions are those concerning our values:

—the responsibilities we have towards future generations;
—human interests and decisions about the environment;
—the moral significance of other forms of sentient life;
—the moral significance of non-sentient forms of life.

To help young people to address questions like these, some attention to education in moral values is required. Values in general are the criteria, meaning, standards or principles, by which we judge 'things' (objects, ideas, actions, people, etc.) to be worthwhile, desirable, or otherwise. In the case of moral values the judgement would concern specific human dispositions and conduct. Dancing is a type of human conduct. Yet when we say that someone is a good dancer we are not usually passing a moral judgement. In order to make that particular judgement we might be appealing to other values, e.g. aesthetic values. Judgements of moral value would include traits of character, actions and ideals which might be termed responsible, blameworthy, despicable, honourable and so on. Judgements of moral value are related ultimately to choices. The fact that something is valued means that it is that 'thing' that is regarded as being worthwhile or desirable as opposed to some other thing, or nothing. A choice is involved. In the context of moral value judgements a person is not usually accorded praise or blame for their judgements if those judgements are the consequence of coercion, compulsion or conditioning for these remove choice. Conversely, a person's values will inform the choices that the person makes, which is not to say that people inevitably choose according to their values. Sometimes, for a variety of reasons, people fall short of their own standards.

Although a person's values will inform the choices that a person makes, this does not mean that everyone has the right to have all of their choices respected regardless of the consequences. Not all choices are of equal worth. This would make the act of choosing pointless. In so far as a value judgement is both a judgement of the worth of a choice and an expression of choice, it is open to scrutiny. First, is the choice congruent with the values it purports to express? Second, is the value itself an expression of what is, in those circumstances, the most appropriate standard or principle?

It follows from these observations that values are not simply feelings. Certainly a value may evoke feelings and those feelings will be part of the meaning of that value. Honesty, generosity and fairness may evoke positive emotions whilst negative emotions are evoked by their opposites. However, when someone says that pollution is wrong, that person is doing more than venting their feelings about pollution. What that person may also be doing is making a series of value judgements such as the following:

- —it is in our interests to have cheap food but this requires a degree of pollution that is accumulative;
- —we aren't the only moral agents involved and have a responsibility to care for future generations;
- —in addition, pollution harms other forms of life which are also morally considerable and, in this context, worthy of equal regard and care.

Although it is in our immediate interests to accommodate a degree of pollution in order to enjoy cheap food, it is not in our longer term interests nor is it in the interests of other forms of life. Therefore, pollution is wrong.

This is not to say that anyone would make these judgements or that these judgements are immune from criticism. However, in so far as anyone could make these judgements, and have them criticised, it becomes clear that they are more than expressions of feeling. Involved in these judgements are values to do with caring, equality and responsibility. They lead to the conclusion that pollution is wrong and they provide reasons for saying so. If someone claimed to espouse these values and yet reached the conclusion that pollution was not wrong there would be grounds to question that conclusion. The values can be prioritised so that caring for people is important but caring for all living things, including people, is even more important because caring for all living things invokes additional values to do with responsibility and equal regard. The person making this judgement has espoused the value, or constellation of values that are, under the circumstances, an expression of the most appropriate standards or principles.

Making value judgements in the manner described invokes two other aspects of choice that should be noted. The first is that the consequences of the choice have to be considered. Thus both providing and not providing cheap food involve consequences which have to be weighed. The second aspect concerns the intentions or motives of the person making the judgement. There is clearly a difference between an intention that is purely self-regarding and one that recognises duties to all living things. There is a difference between selfish and selfless motives. In making value judgements both consequences and intentions may have to be considered.

To make the judgement it is necessary to have a concept of care, equality and responsibility. In this sense too, values are more than feelings. They also have a cognitive dimension. It is also the case that our value judgements are informed by facts. In the example given it would be important to know just how much pollution, and of what kind, people can actually accommodate.

Some conclusions can be drawn about the kinds of abilities that young people need to acquire if they are to make moral judgements. Young people need to be able to:

Identify and clarify the issue – in terms of what is worthwhile or desirable concerning traits of character, actions and/or ideals. This will involve an understanding of the values involved including conceptual clarity about the meaning of those values.

Gather and use information – For the sake of clarity, one will need to know, for example, what the effects of pollution are.

Exercise choice – Given that a range of judgements may reflect that which is worthwhile or desirable in the circumstances and in the light of the relevant information, standards of rationality will be important. The young person will also require understanding of intentions or motives and the capacity to predict the consequences of a choice.

An example of an environmental dilemma is instructive. You live in a part of the country that is the last habitat of a variety of rare plant and animal life, and that lies between a major manufacturing town and a busy port. Existing road links between the town and the port are crowded, unsafe and inefficient. The proposal is to build a new multi-lane highway through this last remaining habitat. A group of activists are planning a campaign of civil disobedience. You sympathise with their cause but you also appreciate the safety and efficiency arguments. What should you do?

Identifying and clarifying the issue will involve weighing a number of competing demands. For example the interests of people are morally considerable. On the one hand, building a new road will create jobs, albeit temporarily. However, the loss of a variety of plant and animal life will ultimately diminish the quality of human life. This loss might be outweighed by gains involving jobs, safety and efficiency. Jobs, safety and efficiency and even natural diversity, in the manner expressed, are all anthropocentric concerns for they reflect human interests. However, if animals or plants have interests that makes them morally considerable in their own right, what is worthwhile or desirable should include the interests of the animals and plants involved. Conceptual clarity about the values involved is vital.

Part of the process of identifying and clarifying the issue will be the use of information. It would be important to have information about jobs, safety, efficiency, animal and plant loss, and what civil disobedience would involve.

Having identified and clarified the issue with the help of the appropriate information a choice of judgement may be made. One may then try to predict consequences and these will, in turn, have a bearing on what is judged to be desirable. Thus, for example, the consequences of engaging in civil disobedience would have to be weighed against the consequences of that action being successful. Intentions or motives will also have a bearing on the judgement. The intention might be to promote a particular human interest but a variety of human interests are at stake. Moreover, there are non-human interests to consider. The dilemma also asks what should be done. This indicates another ability that young people need to acquire:

Engage in an action appropriate to the identified values – This final ability indicates that there is a connection between values and behaviour and that moral values education should help the young person to act.

Moral values education, that addresses environmental issues, can occur everywhere that environmental education occurs. Of more significance is the importance of this work for the school as a whole. Moral values education, if properly conducted, inevitably exposes the values of the school. As the NCC's Guidance Document argues, pupils cannot be expected to value that which is not clearly valued by the school. If the school attaches no value to its own environment then that will be a potent message. Conversely, the school that cherishes its own environment will itself be a resource for moral values education.

POLITICS

Marcus Lyon

At a time when many schools are hard-pressed to find space for all the demands of the National Curriculum, it is important to remember that Politics can contribute to a variety of cross-curricular themes, including Environmental Education. If education is about preparing well-rounded students for the realities of adult life, then we cannot afford to ignore those areas which, whilst neither Core nor Foundation, are still crucial to the development of a responsible citizen. Although dealing predominantly with the links between Politics and Environmental Education in secondary schools, many of the points made below could apply equally to those teaching in the primary sector. It could be argued that only when Politics Education begins at Key Stage 1, will it be possible to fully educate students about their rights, opportunities and responsibilities as citizens.

The level of ignorance about politics, amongst students, is often alarming. In a supposedly democratic state, where we are encouraged to believe that we have direct access to political power, many students leave school with only the vaguest notions of how local and national government works. Whilst they might be confident in describing how certain interest groups can encourage change, they are often confused about how that can then be translated into political action. This is surprising when one considers the degree of interest shown by students in environmental issues. Support for environmental groups, such as Greenpeace and Friends of the Earth, is often widespread amongst children who are not even remotely interested in the Budget deficit or the rate of inflation. This is not because, as some politicians might have it, these students are idealistic. In many ways it is the reverse. Students see environmentalism as being concerned with making practical decisions about the future. A cursory talk with most secondary school students reveals passionate support for such causes as animal rights and an end to global warming. What it will not necessarily demonstrate is any realistic understanding of how to go about implementing change. At Key Stage 3, particularly within what may be called Personal and Social Education, teachers have an ideal opportunity to channel this genuine interest into a study of the political process. Students tend to be less cynical about politics and are keen to learn about how government works if their interest is stimulated by a variety of practical activities.

Learning about how an election works can, and should, be linked to some form of school election. Students, campaigning for a place on a Year or House committee, often bring an enthusiasm for political issues which would put to shame, even the most ardent environmental activist. The political dimension of environmental issues is done most effectively by considering relevant, local matters. A candidate for a School Council election may wish to encourage voters in their form by promising to tackle the question of litter around the school or the setting up of a recycling scheme. Candidates may promise to question senior staff about the use of environmentally-friendly materials within the school or organise charity events to raise funds for a particular environmental cause.

However, links between politics and environmental education at Key Stage 3 can be varied. Most pupils will know that there is a local Member of Parliament but they will probably have no idea about that MP's work or responsibilities. Teaching pupils how to access political power must start by encouraging them to understand the way in which elected representatives go about their business. Practical activities, such as writing mock letters to MPs about issues which concern them, can highlight the fact that they, as future voters, have a major role to play. Better still, we ought to be encouraging the representatives themselves to talk directly to students. Naturally, not all politicians are either willing to do this or are good at it. This in itself will tell students something about the nature of politics. As is generally the case when politicians do accept such engagements, they often find themselves vigorously challenged on a host of environmental issues.

At Key Stage 4 and A level, politics tends to work on two levels with the older pupils. The first of these is an extension of Key Stage 3 within Personal and Social Education, as well as sixth form General Studies. Politics has a vital role to play in broadening the curriculum for students. It often runs in conjunction with some basic form of environmental education programme. Even so, the links to be made between the two disciplines are profound. Most of these older students are actively looking towards the outside world of either work or Further and Higher Education. An understanding of the health and safety laws governing most workplaces is an ideal starting point for a discussion about the ways in which politicians legislate for environmental factors. Those students who go on work experience are brought into daily contact with these factors, and some will even work in areas of environmental interest, such as forestry and land management. Politics, within a PSE programme, can draw out the experiences of students and relate them to the wider arena of policy-making and governmental intervention.

Many older teenagers are also involved in some sort of quasi-political activity. These activities are more often than not linked to environmental causes. They may hand out leaflets about Animal Rights at the weekend or attend anti-nuclear demonstrations. Educators frequently underestimate the amount of active involvement students have in political issues. Tutor time is an ideal opportunity for them to draw out and develop generalisations about politics and environmental issues from the specific experience of their own students.

A more intensive examination of, for example the role of the media in political life, can be undertaken in General Studies A level. Here too it is possible to select examples of environmental issues. The marketing campaigns of environmental groups often give fascinating insights into their political aims and objectives. A study of the political and environmental implications of the recent Earth Summit held in Rio de Janeiro, could be the basis for a thoughtful answer in a General Studies examination. The range of possible links is vast.

The other level at which Politics works in the upper school is at GCSE and A levels. It is here that time can be spent unravelling the intricacies of politics. At examination level students can be encouraged to learn, in detail, about the decision-making processes and their effect upon environmental issues. In the teaching of American Politics, for example, environmental issues can often be brought into the discussion. President Clinton's recent NAFTA victory, and his signalling of a desire for closer links with the Pacific nations, have tremendous implications for the global environment and developing nations. Likewise, the dichotomy between the American Federal government's Clear Air Act of 1990, and the decision of some individual states, such as California, to opt for even tougher legislation, says a great deal about the growing impact of environmentalists on the American political scene. A student who understands something of the lobbying system, as it affects industrial corporations and environmental groups in Washington, has gained a valuable insight into the realities of American political life. In all of these examples, it is possible to explore fruitful connections between Politics and Environmental Education.

Equally, in British politics, it is possible to trace the history of a particular environmental issue from a political perspective. The problem of 'acid rain', which has caused disputes between Britain and such countries as Norway, dates back to the smogs of 1952 and to subsequent, inadequate clean air legislation. As a result, the failure of governments to deal with the emission of sulphur dioxide is still on the agenda. Close beside it is the growing evidence of a link between an increase in asthma sufferers and car exhaust pollution. The action taken by successive governments on this one issue can clarify, for students, a range of political processes. Further issues, such as the adoption of 'green' policies by the major political parties in an effort to secure more votes, can flesh out the student's awareness.

Ideally, students also ought to be encouraged to draw out the links between politics and environmental issues through extended course work. This could be wide-ranging enough so as to develop a theme in detail. Many Politics courses encourage such components and students frequently use them to pursue their environmental interests. The skills gained in both research and analysis will be of benefit to students in both the short and long term.

For the teacher trying to develop Environmental Education across the curriculum, the use of Politics at all stages has tremendous potential. To the students themselves, it can be seen as an immensely enjoyable activity which has a satisfying, practical relevancy. However, coordinators ought never to forget that Politics opens up channels for discussion and learning. It is not an opportunity for indoctrination. Parents in particular, see the negative potential of Politics and are often concerned. They are generally sceptical of the value of political education, just as they remain sceptical about the value of environmental education. Clearly stated aims and objectives, as well as the parameters, of political and environmental education may ensure parental support.

FINANCE

Ian Duffell

Nobody likes waste. Many schools in the UK organise recycling programmes for aluminium cans, waste paper or bottles, but one should be
questioning whether such schemes do more harm than good to the environment. One of the problems is that too few people ever analyse the matter
objectively and, consequently, they tend to confuse the various aims:

—to save money;
—to save resources;
—to protect the environment;
—to make the participants feel better.

Debate in schools may be encouraged by considering each issue in turn, for
they do not have simple answers.

To Save Money

Some readers may remember taking glass bottles back to the shop and collecting a few pennies 'deposit'. The bottles were returned to the
manufacturer to be washed, refilled, relabelled and redistributed. The reason the manufacturer bottled a commodity in the first place was to make a
profit and this system was cost efficient in the 1950's

This system must now be re-evaluated. Bottle manufacturing has greatly
improved so new bottles are cheaper to produce. A much greater diversity
of bottles now exists. If it becomes more expedient, drinks manufacturers
will change to plastic bottles, cans or cartons. Greater diversity of material
available for recycling means increased handling and sorting. Such labour
is probably more expensive than in the 1950's.

Health regulations are now much stricter, so ordinary washing is probably inadequate and will not cope with major contamination. The raw
material for glass is silica or sand and there seems to be no shortage of that.
Allowing for the following costs one must question whether recycling glass
bottles, by even the most modern methods, is cost-effective:

—fuel used going to the bottlebank;
—manufacture of the skip;
—rent of space for the skip;
—lorry to collect the skip;
—energy to melt the glass;
—occasional quality rejects.

If the figures for these costs made the process economically worthwhile
then entrepreneurs would have entered the area with schemes. Add in the
costs of pollution control caused by some of the above factors and one is

beginning to consider the matter objectively.

A similar calculation could be made regarding old newspapers. A local school had set up a waste paper collection centre when the paper could be sold for £24 per ton. Prices are now down to £10 per ton which makes it not worth the time and effort involved and the centre is closing. Germany recently set up a massive waste paper salvage operation creating over-supply so that they began to export their surplus. Europe and the US now have more waste paper than they know what to do with. Again one should consider the transport costs and pollution of collection and processing, especially the environmental damage caused by bleaching the paper.

To Save Resources

It is quite possible for the human race to spoil the earth but one must have a healthy regard for Nature's ability to repair damage. Some years ago a major fire devastated a huge area of rain forest. Everyone thought it was a disaster. Now, five years or so later the following has occurred:

— the ash has fertilised the soil;
— new trees are growing from seed;
— the species mix is greater than before when only tall trees could survive;
— grass is growing and wild flowers have bloomed where it was gloomy before;
— deer and other animals have returned and most traces of the fire have disappeared.

Most paper and cardboard sent for recycling comes from new strains of very fast-growing softwood and whilst a ton of newsprint does take seventeen trees, they are trees grown for the purpose which would otherwise not be grown at all. Nearly all paper comes from farmed trees grown in response to the need for it and no trees are saved by recycling paper. Furthermore, while trees absorb carbon dioxide, they do it most at the growing stage so that harvesting ensures a constant supply of growing trees.

As previously indicated sand is in plentiful supply. In environmental education it is the emotional aspect of running out of resources which should be balanced by the reality that the top mile of the earth's crust is estimated to contain a million times the quantity of minerals in present known reserves, which themselves represent roughly a hundred years' supplies. Even this ignores replacement by technology, e.g. fibre optics for copper in telecommunication cables or nylon for silk in stockings. We are a long way from running out of raw materials.

Iron and steel, clothing and furniture have always been recycled for economic reasons, long before environmentalism came into vogue. Today aluminium cans are worth around 1p each and many schools and youth groups collect them. Although the recycled material uses only 10% of the energy needed to produce aluminium from bauxite ore, an individual would be hard-pressed to make a living by collecting and selling aluminium cans. Aluminium is the most abundant metal on our planet making up some 8% of the earth's crust.

People do not make uneconomic decisions. As soon as something seems to be in short supply, the price rises and demand usually falls and vice versa. A basket of $1,000 of natural resources in November 1980 was worth only $424 in November 1990. If a price continues to rise, then alternatives are sought or research yields extra supplies, e.g. North Sea oil and gas. Natural resources are also becoming less scarce because of constantly improving technology. Rather than use less raw material, the Third World may be helped to emerge from its poverty by the West buying basic raw materials from them.

Packaging often comes in for criticism yet packaging reduces waste. The cost of packaging is less than the cost of spoilage otherwise sustained.

To Protect the Environment

Protecting the environment means different things to different people. Pupils should realise that alarmist news is more exciting than a balanced discussion. Further, it is pointless to advocate a return to past technological levels or lifestyles.

Burning trees is generally deplored yet domestic cooking accounts for 99% of all annual woodburning. Human activity, often seen as the villain of the piece, only accounts for 3.5% of the carbon dioxide produced annually. Termites are a more significant source. Carbon dioxide levels may not be so bad as suggested. The levels were 5 to 10 times higher when dinosaurs roamed the earth. It also seems that global warming might increase vegetation growth which could self-correct carbon dioxide levels although increasing carbon dioxide might counter some of the effects of ozone-depleting CFCs.

Pollution of the air with chemicals can be up to 70 times higher inside homes than outside. Air fresheners, deodorants, hair sprays, mothballs, dry-cleaned clothes, chlorinated drinking water, cigarette smoke, etc. go largely unchecked while lobbyists campaign about the control of car emissions to reduce the risk of diseases caused by breathing polluted air.

The problem with protecting the environment is that human beings do pollute the planet by consuming resources, creating waste and modifying the scenery. If one carried environmental protection to its logical conclusion, one would advocate the end of the human race. More practically, one might suggest limits to population growth, bringing environmental matters into conflict with human rights. The extinction of species has been a biological fact for the last 500 million years. Were it not for the extinction of dinosaurs, the human race might never have evolved.

There is no shortage of landfill sites, in advanced economies, for domestic rubbish because of mining, quarrying and gravel and brick-clay extraction. When exhausted, these voids can be filled, sealed and returned to a usable landscape.

To save the use of fossil or nuclear fuels, wind farms might be built. However 600 windmills, taller than St Paul's Cathedral and covering an area larger than Greater Manchester, could only supply 1% of national electricity needs. The noise would require local residents to be rehoused and large numbers of birds would be killed. Windpower may not be so environmentally-friendly as first thought.

Since the trade in ivory was banned, uncarved elephant tusks rose in price from $2.50 per pound in 1969 to $34 a pound in 1978 and $90 today. In Kenya hunting is banned and poaching rife. In Botswana hunting is permitted on a limited basis, licences being sold at $25,000 per hunt. Local communities have a share of permits which they can sell and they therefore have an interest in not poaching. Economic forces can be an effective means of giving the elephant population a chance of survival.

General Motors have developed a flywheel-powered car that can accelerate to 60 mph in 6.5 seconds, producing no carbon monoxide, lead or dust particles. The engine's battery is charged in six hours from the household mains and will propel the car for up to 600 miles compared to 320 from a petrol-engined vehicle. The cost of the car would be $20,000. The benefits to the environment are clear. Using electricity generated centrally means that pollution control from burning fossil fuels is localised and more effective. British Gas suggest that, with a cost effective modification of around $1,500 per vehicle, natural gas could be used to replace petrol. A test of 300 cars indicates that the fuel is 30% cheaper, emits 30% less carbon dioxide, 70% less carbon monoxide and almost no sulphur or soot particles. These technological advances are largely ignored by a media which seeks sensationalist environmental news.

Tribology

A useful science is that of tribology which involves the study of industrial efficiency which implies saving energy and costs.

For example if a metal part of a car engine wears out it needs to be replaced. A better quality, harder steel would have saved:

—oil burned lubricating the wearing part;
—manufacture of a replacement;
—labour to replace the part;
—fuel and labour to deliver the part;
—manufacture of tools to make the part;
—part of factories for manufacture of the part and tools;
—a part of an iron ore mine;
—a part of a coal mine;

—a part of the mining machines used to provide raw materials – and so on, ripples constantly spreading out.

However one must also consider the effects on employment caused by such reductions. One person's cost is another's income and the whole study can become complex and emotional. There are few simple solutions although one was found in Germany over cleaning up the Rhine. Any factory taking water from the Rhine was made to take it downstream of their own discharge pipe. The effect was quite remarkable.

Green Investments

This area provides challenging material for older pupils. One needs to consider to what extent the investments of a 'Green Unit Trust' are ecologically sound. The level of wages, safety in the factory, competitiveness and its effect upon the future employment of workers all need careful consideration. The appeal to altruistic feelings in 'green investment' advertisements is also interesting. They might be used as an excuse for a 'poor' dividend. Pension funds have to decide whether they are serving their pensioners or the environment. One must be careful to gather legitimate evidence before deciding whether a company is behaving ethically or not. Again there are no simplistic answers for one person's ethical investment may be another's inefficient operation.

Conclusion

All economic activity generates by-products, some of which are unpleasant. It is difficult to measure the value of future damage when we do not know the values of future generations.

Gross National Product growth has improved longevity, diet, health, comfort, hours of work and choice for many people. Material betterment improves the prospects for civilised behaviour. Books, pictures, music, clean air and water and attractive countryside all cost money which must be generated. Pesticides and other chemical aids have meant more efficient production of food. In the past 70 years, potato production has quadrupled and many food costs have fallen. Sales of organic produce in supermarkets are poor with many considering discontinuing their sale as prices are too high.

Finance and Environmental Education should be linked but there are some deeply-held prejudices which have to be challenged. Pollution and capitalist activities have not matched the damage caused by nuclear experiments and planned economies of Eastern European totalitarian states.

The topics are complex, especially if one also takes into account human inconsistency. Many young people believe passionately in saving whales, etc. yet play music loudly, drop litter and so on. A useful discussion could

centre upon these matters considering the suggestion that if no one owns
something, no one protects it.

Pupils should be taught how to see behind beguiling posters. When
schools consider the financial aspects of Environmental Education, their
pupils should learn how to make decisions based upon rational discussion,
logical argument and reputable evidence. If that evidence conflicts with theory, then the theory must yield.

DRAMA

Neil Kitson

Avoiding 'Motorway disasters' – a critical look at the use of contemporary drama methods in environmental education

For teachers of drama in education there is a standard environmental story that is both familiar and dreaded. Known as the 'motorway drama', it can also be about a canal, rain forest or attractive piece of countryside. The only common feature is that the affected community will be divided over issues.

It would appear that children have become involved in the fiction and must, as a result, be involved with the facts. There is, however, little evidence of this. More often the children experience a superficial and non-too-profound lesson. They may converse with a degree of conviction but one must question what they actually learn from environmental education through drama. In drama terms we talk about putting oneself in another's shoes and dealing with the universal issues of life. (Boulton, 1979) One may ask whether it is right to use such terms or whether these universal issues exist in the 'motorway drama'. (Hornbrook, 1993) Teachers must ensure that the issues and teaching objectives are clear. We must use drama in education as a powerful teaching strategy not just as a way of making learning appear more palatable. There is an identified value to drama or it would not appear so regularly in various approaches to environmental education. (ILEA, 1984; Boulton and Kitson, 1989) Children should be guided beyond the superficial to deeper understanding as teachers provide better opportunities than the 'motorway' format.

Taught well, Drama is an excellent way of investigating human relationships with the environment:

> the environment as the common heritage of mankind;
> the common duty of maintaining, protecting and improving the quality of the environment;
> the need for a prudent and rational utilisation of resources;
> the way in which each individual can, by his own behaviour, particularly as a consumer, contribute to the protection of the environment.
>
> (NCC, 1990)

Communication skills, problem-solving skills and positive attitudes towards the environment are promoted. Drama provides the pupils with opportunities for:

> expressing views and ideas about the environment through different media...dramatic...;
> arguing clearly and concisely about environmental issues;
> identifying causes and consequences of environmental problems;
> forming reasoned opinions and developing balanced judgements about environmental issues;

working co-operatively with others;

appreciation of, and care and concern for the environment and for other living things;

independence of thought on environmental issues;

a respect for the beliefs and opinions of others;

a respect for evidence and rational argument;

tolerance and open-mindedness.

(NCC, 1990)

To achieve these goals one first needs to consider the drama process. We are not asking the children to act out a play nor are they living out some notion of reality. The best drama recognises the process for itself. It makes clear to the children that they are making up a story and that none of what goes on is real. It may be very tense and exciting when you confront the group, without letting them know you are making up a drama, by saying something like, 'I've just heard from the headteacher that the council are planning to build a factory on the school field.' The teacher has to know to what extent the children are involved in a drama and quite clearly they are not. What results is anger and a sense of betrayal. Drama is about playing. These children are involved in reality. We must either be other people, in another time or look at the problem from a different perspective in order to establish what Neelands (1990) calls distance through person, time or space. The quality of the interactions will not be significantly diminished by telling the class that they are making up a story about the council building on the school field. However the quality of their reflective learning that can be drawn out from the situation is improved.

To be effective, the teacher must have a clear focus, a learning objective which the drama will consider. Without this focus one may wander in a collective fantasy, being diverted from the main point of the lesson by some minor issue. That is not to say that the children should merely act out the teacher's play. This would be uninspiring. One must be aware of what Morgan and Saxton (1987) have identified as the play for the teacher and the play for the children. Both must exist simultaneously and the skill of the teacher is to integrate the two so that they (the learning focus and the excitement of the story as it unfolds) are seen as one. Drama is a collective process. It is important for the children to recognise it as such. Children and teacher must collaborate to maximise the learning potential offered by drama.

One deficiency in the 'motorway drama' is its lack of depth. When exploring environmental issues we often expect children to care passionately about something to which they are totally indifferent. Children can operate at a superficial level, satisfying the teacher's need for them to be on task using language or occupational mime. In drama we are trying to encourage the children to think and act 'as-if' they are the people in the fiction, feeling and reacting accordingly. (Weininger, 1988) We do not want them to work in a superficial, conscious mode whereby they are thinking, 'what if' I was a protester, how would I stand, speak and look? These two conditions have been explored by Singer and Singer (1989) who quite clearly see the 'what if' state as being socio-dramatic play whereas the 'as-if' state is drama. The problem for teachers using drama is how to attain the deeper state. Heathcote (1979) indicates the key is commitment and belief. It does not matter what the issue is, it is hard to feel any relationship towards it if one is not interested in it. If we want the children to respond we must help them build commitment and belief.

When exploring environmental issues using dramatic techniques we must go beyond role-play. Drama is very effective when used in the appropriate situation but the problem arises with regards to its excessive and indiscriminate use. As Boulton and Kitson (1989) point out, whilst role-play is drama, there is much more to drama than role-play. Its inappropriate use has led to it being devalued in the eyes of the pupils. The best dramas have a beginning where we find out who we are, where we are and what's up, a series of complications to the story, a climax and a final stage where loose ends are dealt with. All too often dramas linked to an environmental theme miss out the important first two stages and begin with conventions appropriate for the climactic phase. (Neelands, 1990) As a result we end up with a 'motorway' debate that no one really cares about. Far better to start off by defining the community with each child saying something about their role in the village, a significant moment in village life or putting someone in the 'hot seat' in order to find out what it means to live in the community. The debate will then be more meaningful. Even in this simple example we can provide pupils with quality opportunities for:

> arguing clearly and concisely about an environmental issue, identifying causes and consequences of environmental problems and forming reasoned opinions and developing balanced judgements about environmental issues.

> (NCC, 1990)

Drama is not a panacea that makes all learning easier to bear. It is a useful teaching strategy and should be given equal value along with other teaching strategies. In the context of environmental education, drama has a significant role in the teaching of skills, attitudes and understanding. To maximise drama's effectiveness in this area we need to use it with thought. We must help the pupils use drama to explore, for themselves, how the world looks to other people and what responsibilities we have. To achieve this we must consider:

—psychological distance for the children so that they feel safe;
—depth, so that they can become committed;
—belief in the work combined with a focus for the learning area covered;
—a wide range of dramatic techniques which provide the most effective way to match artistic and learning outcomes.

Without such consideration, lessons that employ drama structures run the risk of being arid with the pupils engaged in either active English or fantasy play.

References

Boulton, G. (1979) *Towards a Theory of Drama in Education*. London: Longmans.
Boulton, J.A. and Kitson, N.G. (1989) 'Not another Role-play'. *Humanities Magazine*, **Vol.5**.
Hornbrook, D. (1993) *Education in Drama*. Oxford: Blackwell.
ILEA (1984) *The Wasteground*. London: Inner London Education Authority.
Morgan, N. and Saxton, J. (1987) *Teaching Drama*. London: Hutchinson.
NCC (1990) *Curriculum Guidance 7: Environmental Education*. York: National Curriculum Council.
Neelands, J. (1990) *Structuring Drama Work*. Cambridge: Cambridge University Press.
Singer, D.G and Singer, J.L. (1989) *The House of Make Believe*. Massachusetts: Harvard University Press.
Wagner, B.J. (1979) *Dorothy Heathcote: Drama as a Learning Medium*. London: Hutchinson.
Weininger, O. (1988)' 'What If' and 'As-If': Imagination and Pretend Play in Early Childhood' in *Imagination and Education*. Oxford: Oxford University Press.

SOCIAL SCIENCES

Tony Lawson

The inclusion of Environmental Education in the cross-curricular themes of the National Curriculum is unsurprising. Concern for the environment and the relationship between human beings and nature has been a recurrent political and social issue throughout the twentieth century. Moreover, the increasing globalisation of threats to the environment, in the shape of, for example, the depletion of the ozone layer or the widespread radiation poisoning which followed the disaster at Chernobyl, has intensified that concern. It is therefore entirely laudable that environmental education should be promoted as an aspect of the National Curriculum. However, as with the other cross-curricular themes, the relationship of the social sciences, and, in particular, sociology and psychology, to environmental education is problematic. This is partly because the social sciences stand outside the defined subject areas of the National Curriculum, but also because the definition of social sciences in the National Curriculum documentation is restricted.

Yet the aims of environmental education as detailed in *Curriculum Guidance 7* specifically encourage a social scientific contribution:

> encourage pupils to examine and interpret the environment from a variety of perspectives – physical, geographical, biological, sociological, economic, political, technological, historical, aesthetic, ethical and spiritual.

> (NCC, 1990a).

However, the guidance document does not go on to detail in any systematic way what that contribution might be. Rather, there is a series of issues identified throughout the document, which have a vaguely social sciences aspect. For example 'people and their communities' are referred to in the contribution of the National Curriculum subjects (NCC, 1990b) or 'home and family, school, neighbourhood and peer group' when referring to activities that affect the environment which children might already be involved in. Beyond this, there are only general references to the contribution of subjects outside the National Curriculum, or snippets of social scientific concerns such as 'leisure', 'technology' or 'development' in the illustrations used (NCC, 1990c).

The problem here is not just that the social sciences are apparently marginalised in *Curriculum Guidance 7*, but that the lack of any serious input from the social sciences is likely to defeat the whole point of having Environmental Education as a cross-curricular theme in the first place. Ministers of Education and commentators alike have pointed out that environmental education is concerned with more than just knowledge about the environment. It is also about understanding the complexities of the factors which might inflict environmental damage and about involving young people in taking action towards the environment's conservation and improvement. As Norman Farmer wrote:

> Being reasonably satisfied that the core and foundation subjects will provide knowledge about the environment, we must look to those activities that transform a pupil's learning into an education. For Environmental Education, these are first-hand experiences (e.g. fieldwork)...

(Farmer, 1990)

However, it is questionable whether fieldwork on its own can transform learning into an education. Angela Rumbold, when Minister of State for Education and Science, clearly recognised the necessity to go beyond the personal and the immediate:

> Good environmental education...must lead pupils and students out and on from their immediate perceptions and experiences to a wider understanding. It must develop their capacity to go beyond the anecdotal and the particular. None of this happens by chance.

(Rumbold, 1989)

As the traditional task of the social sciences has been to achieve such wider understanding, this statement represents a powerful, if unmeant, plea for the social sciences to be involved in Environmental Education. Indeed, it could be argued that the social sciences could be employed as the organising principle behind the delivery of Environmental Education and thus avoid the

> real danger...that Environmental Education...will be declared to be 'done' by ticking off a collection of attainment targets which sound appropriate, but which are delivered with minimal coherence across a range of traditional 'subjects'.

(Hawkins, 1991)

However, one must consider what the social sciences, as broadly defined, offer in the way of an organising principle for the delivery of Environmental Education. It is the ability of the social sciences to place environmental issues in their political, economic and social contexts which is the distinctive contribution that the social sciences can make. Without such contexts, the possibility of effecting social change concerning the environment is likely to be severely curtailed and environmental education will not achieve its aim of a 'fully informed and active participation of the individual in the protection of the environment' (NCC, 1990a).

More specifically, sociology and to a lesser extent psychology have themselves been concerned with environmental issues, through their consideration of the process of development and its impact on the human environment. While there is an argument that social scientists have usually ignored environmental issues (Redclift, 1987), the classical sociologists did explore the relationship between nature and society in considering the process of modernisation and the social and environmental effects of the transition from a rural to an industrial society. This concern with environmental issues can be traced through the Chicago School and their emphasis on 'Ecology' (Park, 1952) to new sociological developments such as 'Ecofeminism' (Mellor, 1992). Therefore, it could be argued that, while the environment has not been a central area of social scientific investigation in an explicit way, there has been an awareness of the relationship between society, the individual and the environment from the very beginnings of social scientific study.

However, during the 1980's, sociological interest in the environment has been heightened because of a series of developments both within the discipline and in global society itself. Firstly, there has been an increasing tendency for sociology to cross-fertilise with other disciplines in looking at issues with which they are all concerned. For example, when Canter et al. define what they see as the environmental social sciences, they identify 'the domains of Behaviour and Perceptual Geography, Environmental Psychology, Urban Sociology, Social Anthropology, Urban History, Social Ecology, Behavioural Archaeology, Landscapes Architecture and various aspects of design' (Canter et al., 1988) as contributing disciplines.

Secondly, global interest in the environmental aspects of development has been aroused following the United Nations' Conference on the Environment and Development in Rio de Janeiro in June 1992, which put forward Agenda 21: 'a blueprint for a global partnership...It is a bold mandate for change, a call for a fundamental reform in our economic behaviour, based on a new understanding and awareness of the impact of human activity on the environment.' (United Nations, 1993). Central to this understanding are five types of environmental side-effects of development, including number 5 'Social distribution: of which congestion and the loss of a sense of community are examples.' (United Nations, 1971).

Lastly, some sociologists have been increasingly interested in environmental issues and have responded to the call from Dunlap and Catton (1980) for a new 'ecological paradigm.' They have largely rejected the assumptions of modernism to embrace, in varying degrees, a post-modernist distrust of science and technology. For example, Giddens argues that, in contemporary society, individuals exist in a state of anxiety, because contemporary societies are societies of high 'risk'. Important amongst the risks that individuals face is the sense of impending environmental destruction, which has emerged from the activities of science and technology (Giddens, 1990 and 1991).

It is therefore an appropriate time for social scientists in schools and colleges to look again at Environmental Education and seek to provide the necessary context for their students to gain the understanding needed to develop the 'social responsibility' (NCC, 1990b) towards environmental issues which *Curriculum Guidance 7* believes is important.

References

Canter, D., Krampen, M. and Stea, D. (1988) *Environmental Perspectives*. Aldershot: Gower.

Dunlap, R. and Catton, W. (1980) 'A new ecological paradigm for a post-exuberant sociology' *American Behavioural Scientist*, **Vol.24**, No.1.

Farmer, N. (1991) 'Ten tasks for the Implementation of Curriculum Guidance Seven' *Environmental Education*, **37**, Summer (p.9).

Giddens, A. (1990 and 1991) *The Consequences of Modernity*. Oxford: Polity.

Hawkins, G. (1991) 'CG7: Points of view 1: Knowledge and the whole Curriculum' *Streetwise*, **5**, Winter (p.5).

Mellor, M. (1992) *Breaking the boundaries. Towards a Feminist Green Socialism.* London: Virago.

NCC (1990) *Environmental Education: Curriculum Guidance 7*. York: National Curriculum Council. (Section 2; (b) Section 3; (c) Section 5).

Park, R.E. (1952) *Human Communities: The City and Human Ecology.* London: Free Press.

Redclift, M. (1991) *Sustainable Development: Exploring the Contradictions.* London: Routledge.

Rumbold, A. (1989) 'Speech to London International Youth Service Fortnight on 27 July' *Environmental Education*, **32**, Autumn (p.5).

United Nations (1971) Development and Environment: Report of a Panel of Experts convened by the Secretary-General of the United Nations Conference on the Human Environment in Founex, Switzerland, 4-12 June. York: United Nations.

United Nations (1993) *The Global Partnership for Environment and Development: a guide to Agenda 21.* New York: United Nations.

LAW

Don Rowe

In the real world, as opposed to the artificially constructed curriculum world, the relationship between environmental control and the law is a close one. It is by means of legislation that government implements its policies for the environment, however adequate or inadequate these happen to be. Therefore there are many opportunities for teaching pupils about the environment and the nature of law. One significant advantage of this is that environmental issues demonstrate very clearly that the law itself may not represent the easy consensus often pictured in textbooks on citizenship. More often it is a compromise between opposing interests which remain in tension. The law may even represent a situation in which the immediate interests of industry and commerce can be seen to have prevailed over the longer term environmental ones.

Environmental education and law-related education are relative newcomers to the curriculum and are both now widely recognised as essential elements of the entitlement curriculum. Law-related education (LRE) can be defined as the process of teaching and learning about the role of law in society as it affects ordinary citizens (NCC, 1990a; Rowe, 1992). LRE attempts to empower citizens by informing them about the extent of their legal rights and duties and how law works as an instrument of social policy. Law-related education also seeks to encourage the development of a 'critical solidarity' stance, viz-a-viz legislation. This is to say that, in a democracy, one of the prime functions of citizens is to criticise existing legislation and, directly or indirectly, to bring pressure to bear on politicians to respond to changing social and ecological needs.

To argue the link between environmental and law-related education is relatively non-problematic. But there is always a gap (sometimes amounting to a chasm) between educational rhetoric and classroom practice. Every teacher is now familiar with the rhetoric of cross-curricularity. It is frequently generalised and exhortative in style yet many of the difficulties of making such links are glossed over. Quite apart from the question of teacher skill and confidence, there is often a more fundamental problem arising from the nature of the different subjects being linked. To take an example relevant to this present discussion in *Curriculum Guidance 3* (NCC, 1990b), the document states that, at one end of the spectrum, the cross-curricular themes: 'can be separately timetabled, at the other end they can be completely subsumed within the subjects of the curriculum. Environmental education, for example, could well be covered in science, geography, technology, English and mathematics.' The implication of this passage seems to be that the whole of what might reasonably be conceived of as 'environmental education' can be apportioned out amongst the mainstream national curriculum subjects. But, if such infusion is to be satisfactory and not cosmetic, it must be done in such a way that its central concerns are addressed in a sufficiently holistic manner as to do it justice in its own right. Cross-curricula delivery raises questions both of 'coverage' and of 'quality'.

It is immediately obvious that a policy of curriculum infusion would not, in fact, be able to examine environmental issues in many of their social, economic, political and legal contexts. Furthermore, reliance on infusion alone, would increase the likelihood that environmental issues are taken up only in passing, or not at all.

The infusion model of cross-curricularity has developed at least partly as a response to the historic weakness of the English curriculum so far as the social sciences and humanities are concerned and this structural weakness continues to undermine many socially important curriculum innovations including environmental and law-related education.

In *Curriculum Guidance 7* (1990c) one of the central objectives of environmental education is described as knowledge and understanding of 'local, national and international legislative controls to protect and manage the environment: how policies and decisions are made about the environment.' Related objectives refer to 'the conflicts which can arise about environmental issues' and 'the importance of effective action to protect and manage the environment'. This requires at least a basic understanding of the nature and role of law in society. For example, pupils should know how legislation is framed and the nature of the powers given by Parliament to ministers of the Crown. In addition, pupils should understand how and why citizens can appeal against government decisions or work to change the law. That is nothing less than their democratic right. But the infusion method of curriculum delivery (as applied to citizenship) would very probably have left pupils ignorant of such background knowledge. It is no more reasonable to ask teachers of environmental education to be responsible for delivering these core elements of law-related citizenship any more than we would expect a physics teacher to have to break off a lesson on forces to teach equations. Thus law-related education should be seen as an essential 'service' subject for the whole of the humanities curriculum, including environmental education. If all this is accepted as reasonable in theory, then it is also important to acknowledge that the reality is very different. What strikes one, when reviewing many environmental resources, is how often this environment/law nexus is overlooked or, at best, left unexploited.

Teachers reading this may feel that it is quite unrealistic for them, as non-experts, to know what the law says on environmental issues in any detail. For example one might need to know who, and under what circumstances, can pollute our rivers or emit sulphur into the atmosphere. Much of this knowledge is necessary before pupils can ask why this is allowed to happen. Most of the interest groups active in this area have education or publicity officers who are willing to provide information of this kind, and they can usually offer examples of how the law works in practice. They may quote case studies of when the law was enforced or challenged. Thus a law-related perspective enables an often generalised debate about an issue to become focussed on the real world of compromise, half measures, and injustice as well as showing pupils how important the legal controls actually are.

It is not only for older pupils that a law-related perspective can be valuable. In *Curriculum Guidance 7*, for example, a case study is offered in which Key Stage 2 pupils investigated the issue of gassing badgers in the fight against bovine tuberculosis. The objectives listed include coverage of legislative controls to protect and manage the environment. During the course of their researches, pupils wrote to various organisations including the Ministry of Agriculture and conservation societies and no doubt discovered what the current legal status of the badger is, as a protected species. At such a point one may ask the children whether the law should be changed. Teachers who might have held a general class debate might instead consider the advantages of debating this kind of issue in the form of a parliamentary bill.

There are several advantages in using this format. First, the issue can be aired generally (the equivalent of the second reading). Then the subject can be taken clause by clause, allowing a much more detailed examination of the issues than the usual debate format. The reason for this is that law needs to be both clear, workable and give due consideration to a multiplicity of conflicting interests. Primary school pupils can well understand many of these detailed aspects if they are presented in the right way and at an appropriate level. For example, imagine that a class has agreed that, in principle, gassing badgers is to be allowed. In an ordinary debate that would be the end of the matter but the 'draft bill' format opens up the need to discuss a number of further issues such as who should be allowed to gas them. Children will quickly see reasons for the decision not being left entirely to the farmer. They may also see the need to prevent 'control' from becoming 'extermination'. The potential of LRE to develop critical and logical reasoning is immense. Using the law as both a resource and a vehicle, it is possible to address a wide range of environmentally crucial questions relating to the rights and responsibilities of citizens, the power of the state and the nature and values of our society (see, for example, Rowe and Thorpe, 1993). Used consistently in this way, the law itself will become less invisible to the next generation of citizens and be viewed as a powerful, omnipresent factor in the creation and re-creation of our social structures.

References

NCC (1990a) *Curriculum Guidance 8: Education for Citizenship*. York: National Curriculum Council.

NCC (1990b) *Curriculum Guidance 3: The Whole Curriculum*. York: National Curriculum Council (p.6).

NCC (1990c) *Curriculum Guidance 7: Environmental Education*. York: National Curriculum Council (p.4).

Rowe, D. (1992) 'Law-related Education: an Overview in Cultural Diversity and the School' in Modgil, S., Modgil, C. and Lynch, J. *Law-related Education*, **Vol.4**. London: Falmer Press (pp.69-86).

Rowe, D. and Thorpe, T. (1990) *Understand the Law, Book 1*. London: Hodder and Stoughton.

Rowe, D. and Thorpe, T. (1993) *Living with the Law, Book 2 'In the Community'*. London: Hodder and Stoughton.

COMMUNICATION AND THE MEDIA

David Blake

A vast amount of information conveyed to us, individually and collectively, is through the forms and technologies of the media. If pupils are to have an informed concern for environmental issues, they need to broaden and deepen their knowledge and experiences in order to come to a wider understanding of what this implies. It is the media that produces the representations on which much of this development is based.

Environmental issues of genuine concern to young people are often presented in the media, sometimes with very extensive coverage. To be able to judge the validity of the information they receive, students need to understand the nature of communication and the techniques that can be used to inform and influence audiences. One aim is to demonstrate that the language of every medium is not natural or neutral.

National Curriculum Guidance 3: The Whole Curriculum identifies six cross-curricular skills: communication, numeracy, study skills, problem-solving, personal and social skills, and those relating to information technology. (NCC, 1990a) It gives examples of how these can be related to environmental education and it is apparent how integral is the part media education has to play in the development of these skills in this context. For example, the study skills section includes 'retrieving, analysing, interpreting and evaluating information about the environment from a variety of sources'. Problem-solving skills include 'forming reasoned opinions and developing balanced judgements about environmental issues'.

As well as encouraging progress with skills, media education also has a key role in the development of attitudes. Independence of thought, recognition of the beliefs and opinions of others, and a respect for evidence and rational argument can be encouraged through the examination and interpretation of media texts. Study of the media requires consideration of the source of ideas and information rather than the passive acceptance of what is presented.

The understanding of media agencies, languages and representations shares common ground with certain areas within communication studies. Students can become aware of how a communicator selects the message to be transmitted to the audience and how content and form of presentation are chosen. The communicator will be influenced by ideology and perceptions of the audience; the way the audience receives and makes meaning of the message will be affected by perceptions about the communicator's knowledge and trustworthiness.

> ...the key issue...is the development of an understanding about what difference it might make to the meaning, significance or authenticity of a text if it is made by say, Touchstone rather than by Zenith, or financed by British Nuclear Fuels rather than Greenpeace. (British Film Institute, 1991)

Communication and media studies provide opportunities to examine attitudes. What we believe or know about the subject under consideration, the cognitive component, is obviously important. So, too, is the affective element. Many environmental issues arouse strong emotional responses, some of which may lead to changes in behaviour. Where an individual's change in attitude is translated into positive action, there is the possibility of fulfilling one major aim of environmental education, active participation in resolving problems.

The totality of media output about environmental issues is considerable. In one issue (27 March 1994), *The Observer* included four separate features on such themes. These articles were about: a new plan to make nuclear waste safe; countering the rise in the planet's disappearing plants and animals; measures to make business cost-effective as well as environmentally friendly, and DIY chain stores' commitment to sell only 'sustainably grown' wood. On the same day, six full pages in the *Sunday Express* were given over to a feature about global warming and the *Sunday Telegraph* reported on plans to curtail erosion of footpaths in the Lake District.

In addition, BBC2 showed a 30 minute programme about protecting flood plains and the press contained reviews of film and video releases with themes based on the conservation of the earth's resources. The quality is not, however, consistent. *On Deadly Ground*, a film in which an oil-rig worker challenges his employer over pollution in Alaska was described as having dialogue which is 'truly toxic'! On the contrary, *Ferngully...The Last Rainforest* was praised for the style in which it delivers an ecological warning.

The British Film Institute suggests that media education must address the totality of children's cultural experience. There is a tendency to focus on informational and persuasive forms, less heed being paid to fictional and entertainment ones. These, too, contribute to knowledge of the world, different areas, groups, attitudes, economies and environments. Children need to understand how ideas and meanings are constructed in different media and in different genres.

There are case studies of projects in which learning objectives for both environmental education and study of the media have been successfully met. Two are described in *Media Education: an introduction.* (Alvarado and Boyd-Barrett, 1992)

The first was completed by a class of Year 3 pupils in an inner city Leeds school. The focus was on visual representations and extended the children's experience of decoding photographic images. Pupils then took their own photographs in the local park. Some of them were designated to show it as a pleasant place, some unpleasant. Awareness was raised of issues relating to the local environment and there was an increased level of understanding of the media element.

The second project was based on the care of trees, a subject relevant to the school involved and also an issue of wider concern. The 19 pupil primary school produced a video programme. The technology gave them the means to communicate their views and the unit of work illustrated how media empowers, making it possible to influence others.

Secondary Media Education: A Curriculum Statement contains a summary of a Year 10 project, 'The World Food Problem'. Students were shown how to recognise media devices, such as the narrative behind images, and discussed how preconceptions can be exploited by media agencies. By examining material from numerous sources, they learned how to deconstruct and decode media output.

Environmental education raises issues and creates opportunities to extend experience. It provides meaningful and important contexts for activities in which attitudes can be refined and skills enhanced. In whatever subject area the environment is being studied, there will be the need to refer to a range of secondary sources, such as television programmes, photographs, films, maps, documents and books. Media education and communication studies enable students to understand and appreciate the knowledge, attitudes and values within each of these texts.

However, the place of the study of the media within the National Curriculum is under threat. The Dearing Review has undertaken to reduce statutory requirements and media study has lost ground in previous processes of rationalisation within statutory orders.

English for Ages 5–11 (the first Cox Report, 1988) saw benefits for pupils through the application of their critical faculties and the focus on 'language, interpretation and meaning'. It was recognised that in the secondary school media studies may exist discretely, as well as being embedded elsewhere in the curriculum. The orders for English were considered the most appropriate ones in which to include media education, given common aims about exploring language, interpretation and meaning.

The statutory orders were published in March 1990 with *Attainment Target 2, Reading*, containing the elements of media education. *Non-Statutory Guidance* (June 1990) included a media education section (D16-20), which contains suggested approaches. It also gives exemplar units of work, one of which is the *Local Area*, a module with an environmental education focus.

Proposals for revised orders for English were published in April 1993. These were intended to reduce English to its essential core and media education was virtually omitted. This fact was commented upon as a particular concern by 14% of the respondents during the consultation period (NCC *Consultation Report: English*, September 1993). Reports suggest specific guidance will be produced for teachers by the subject advisory team designing the revised orders.

The future status of media education in the prescribed curriculum may be as a peripheral element. Thus far, its value has not been fully recognised in the National Curriculum, with a piecemeal rather than coherent approach. It has been left to such bodies as the British Film Institute to suggest structures and frameworks which can ensure progression in the development of skills and understanding. Committed schools and teachers will obviously continue with successful practice, however little reference is made in statutory orders.

The aims of environmental education are fundamental to the quality of life now and in the future. They include the acquisition of knowledge and values, the development of skills of examination and analysis and a growing awareness and commitment that leads to active participation. The marginalisation of media education in statutory curriculum orders is occurring at a time when more information is being transmitted in ways which demand thorough interpretation. It is and will remain, an essential part of effective environmental education.

References

Alvarado, M. and Boyd-Barrett, O. (1992) *Media Education: an introduction.* London: British Film Institute.

BFI (1991) *Secondary Media Education: A Curriculum Statement.* London: British Film Institute.

Cox (1988) *English for all Ages 5–11.* London: HMSO, 14.4.

NCC (1990) *National Curriculum Guidance Document Number 3: The Whole Curriculum.* York: National Curriculum Council (p.6).

128

RECORDS OF ACHIEVEMENT

Ian Curtis

Young people have a rare enthusiasm for environmental causes. Such issues stimulate their imaginations and challenge their sense of justice and fairness. They speak knowledgeably about the damage to the ozone layer often long before they understand what ozone is; or of the destructive potential of the motor car before they know what a gas is, harmful or otherwise. Environmental damage is seen as instinctively wrong just as killing animals or throwing down litter is wrong. Understanding why it may be wrong usually comes later. They have little patience with the 'ifs' and 'buts' arguments which seek to justify particular forms of action. They are not easily swayed by viewpoints which appear to support the polluter or the environmental exploiter. It is sometimes argued that these concerns are transient and fashionable, the result of manipulation by the media, and that consequently their impact is shallow and short-lived. However, to dismiss all issues as such is to fail to recognise the extent of threats to the future of the planet which affront children's sense of fairness and may cause foreboding about their own futures.

Hearing seven year olds talk with passion about the need to protect woodlands is a refreshing experience. In a very real way those children are saying something about their future. It is not naive idealism that guides their thinking but a picture of the future that they want. For that reason, pupils' voices are some of the most important in any debate on the environment.

Educators have been effective in helping young people to learn from, and about, the environment. (NCC, 1990a) This learning may not always be particularly coherent or structured but at least it has left many young people with a clearer understanding about the world that they inhabit. Where there has perhaps been less success is in educating for the environment. Educating for the environment involves the consideration of moral and social issues which are themselves complex and controversial. They also present the educator with specific dilemmas in the way in which they are to be presented and offered for discussion. Talking deploringly about the loss of the rain forest is one thing: helping young people to appreciate the social and economic conditions which impel the farmers and loggers to exploit the forests is a challenge of a different order. If pupils are to form a balanced view of the process of forest depletion it is important that these factors are considered.

In a school curriculum which is increasingly restricted to a pragmatic definition of appropriate skills and knowledge, opportunities to educate for the environment are limited. As one of the cross-curricular themes in the National Curriculum, environmental education inevitably enjoys a lower profile for many teachers than the curriculum subjects. This is in spite of the foreword to the National Curriculum Council's guidance document endorsing it as 'an essential part of every pupil's curriculum'. (NCC, 1990b) Being a cross-curricular theme there are no specific subject statements which identify by which a pupil's progress may be assessed. True, there are statements in science and geography which refer directly to an understanding of environmental phenomena as in 'know that human activity may produce changes in the environment that can affect plants and animals' (HMSO, 1991) but there is no coherent framework against which a pupil's developing knowledge of the environment can be measured.

This is not a weakness. If the study of environmental issues is, as has been argued, such a complex one involving the consideration of social and ethical issues, one may question whether any system of assessment and record keeping is possible. But it is instructive to consider what might happen if no such system existed in a school. In the absence of a means of assessing and recording the learner's progress in the acquisition of environmental concepts there is the danger that new learning will be presented in an incoherent and random manner. There is less likelihood that knowledge and skills will be built up progressively and, as a result, the learner's environmental awareness could become a ragbag of confused and contradictory concepts and ideas. However, a formal assessment programme which depends solely on a series of discrete statements, whether drawn from the National Curriculum or not, may also miss vital pieces of information about a learner's understanding. This may be because what is assessed is unrelated to those areas of knowledge which are of greatest significance to that learner. Any system which reduces the complexity of the environment to a number of digestible but weakly related concepts and pieces of information is unlikely to capture the fullness of the learner's understanding.

What is required, therefore, is a system which is sufficiently rigorous to provide a framework for the recording of achievement in a number of skills and areas of knowledge yet flexible enough to allow for learners to demonstrate the fullness of their own achievements in the manner most appropriate to them. A Record of Achievement can provide such a model. Put simply a Record of Achievement is a folder or file in which various assessments of a learner's work, skills, abilities and personal qualities are collated accumulatively. It fulfils four principle purposes:

—the recognition of achievement, by providing teachers and pupils with an opportunity to give recognition to achievements in a broad range of experiences;
—the enhancement of motivation and personal development by encouraging perseverance and the development of pupils' talents and interests through that recognition;
—the organisation of the curriculum and learning;
—the Record of Achievement process provides comprehensive and detailed information from which the school and pupil can plan the next learning experience; it is a document in which these attainments

and achievements are recorded and which can be regularly updated and reviewed.

The record does not confine itself, therefore, to the work and experiences that the learner has in the school. It provides a much fuller picture of their interests and achievements so that anyone reading it has a more complete view of the learner's competencies. Through the Record of Achievement recognition is given to those many areas of involvement which may otherwise have been missed or ignored. For example many children become involved in environmental projects in the outside community. If this activity is unknown to the teacher, then the opportunity to take the experiences gained into account in planning future work may be missed.

Frequently it is the learners who retain editorial control over what goes into the Record. This provides a mechanism for them to indicate what they feel to be the more relevant and significant aspects of their work. It also provides the teacher with an insight into the pattern of reasoning being adopted by the learner, an understanding which can be further explored in the dialogue and negotiation which forms an important part of the process. There is no one standard method of completing a Record of Achievement and this lack of a prescriptive format also encourages flexibility in what is recorded. By having access to a wide variety of types of recording device the learner may demonstrate, through the Record of Achievement, levels of understanding which are difficult to record by other more rigid means.

The compilation of the record also allows the learner and the teacher to discuss progress together and, through this discussion, the teacher is able to investigate the learner's level of understanding or commitment to that aspect of their learning. Records of Achievement also often lead to learners engaging more fully in their own assessment. By asking questions of themselves they confront those areas of their knowledge which are less secure.

The Record of Achievement is built up cumulatively and shows the progression of a developing interest or skill. By referring to it the teacher or parent is able to form a picture of how that development has proceeded. Some pupils leave school to pursue careers where a knowledge of environmental issues and causes is of considerable benefit. The employer, seeking evidence of such knowledge, will find it in a thoughtfully developed Record of Achievement. The evidence may be in a variety of forms. Examples could include diaries of work on conservation projects or certificates showing involvement in litter-picking activities. Entries of this nature provide the prospective employer with an indication of the true level of a pupil's commitment.

However, Records of Achievement in practice have their problems. Whilst they can be a potent source of motivation they can, if not developed sympathetically, also become an unremitting chore. The young person required to go through the ritual of completing entries for the Record of Achievement when there is little of significance to record can quickly become disenchanted and, instead of being further stimulated and motivated by the process, react with antipathy towards the subject being studied. Similarly for some the record can become one, not of achievement, but of non-achievement and failure to succeed which can further erode self-confidence and esteem.

Whilst these potential hazards must be borne in mind the value of a Record of Achievement to the environmental educator is considerable. It provides a process by which the totality of the learner's knowledge and understanding can be judged and information from a number of areas of the learner's experience synthesised. Perhaps most importantly, it offers a means by which an interest and enthusiasm for the environment can be nourished. For the future well being of the planet it is crucial that the passion for the environment felt by young people is not dissipated by sterile teaching and learning. Any method that depends on the active participation of the learner in the acquisition and retention of an understanding of environmental issues merits consideration, particularly at a time when there are so many other areas of study competing in an otherwise greatly overloaded curriculum.

References

HMSO (1991) *Science in the National Curriculum*. London: HMSO.
NCC (1990a) *National Curriculum Guidance 7; Environmental Education*. York: National Curriculum Council ((b)p.4).

COMMUNITY EDUCATION

Terry Bull

The links between community education on the one hand and an under-standing of the nature of environmental education on the other are both complex and powerful. Environmental education is, in a very real sense, an integral part of that demanding and exciting pedagogical orientation commonly called community education.

The issues raised by this claim are useful ones to consider and argument about them might help readers to clarify their understanding of these two themes which must be kept to the forefront of educational discourse and action.

There are four principal ways in which community education maintains its supremacy:

- by keeping environmental considerations keyed into such educational issues as equality of opportunity, empowerment and relevance in the curriculum;
- it keeps environmental approaches realistic by encouraging development outwards from the problems and needs of individuals, groups and communities to the wider global issues;
- it strives to enlist all social classes and ethnic groups to the view that constructive discontent with the way we handle one another and the globe is a vital powerhouse for local and world wide survival;
- it maintains a kind of quality control by ensuring that aspects on each curriculum are relevant, appropriate and sensitive to the lives and needs of the target groups concerned.

There is a simple framework associated with each of the two areas in question which can, perhaps, be used to demonstrate the nature of the relationship. One may suggest four headings which summarize the aims of community orientated activity in schools. Then there are three frequently used summarizing categories for environmental education.

Community Education
- Promotion of the ideas of community and community spirit and the regeneration of aspects of behaviour associated with them.
- Promotion of the idea of education as a lifelong process.
- Achievement of equality of opportunity.
- Development of inter-cultural sensitivity, empathy and harmony.

Environmental Education
- Education **about** the environment.
- Education **for** the environment.

• Education **through** the environment.

In their approaches to education **about** the environment community educators seek to maximize the immediate relevance to the children of the activities. The intention is to give them the information and skills which will help them to gain control over their own lives and destinies, and enable them to become sensitive, participating and influential members of their immediate, and wider, community. They also seek to adjust the content and approach to the nature of the community served by the school. In a disadvantaged catchment area methods would be used which took pains to validate the life experiences and language of local families. In this way cultural barriers between the school and its curriculum, on the one hand and the cultures served by the school, on the other hand are lowered. The resulting 'user friendly' structure loses some of the arrogance inherent in the middle class imposition of environmental topics far removed from some parents' very real worries about maintaining a reasonable life for their children in a relatively hostile environment. The involvement of parents in the process, which would certainly be promoted by community educators, would bring a reality and continuing education aspect to the work.

For example a project on 'Birds in our Neighbourhood' becomes part of a wider topic called, 'Migration'. In an inner city school such a topic might cover such aspects as:

(1) When families arrived in the neighbourhood and where they came from. Contributions here from parents, orally and, perhaps, in print if the school has resources to produce booklets written by parents.
(2) Similar studies of the wildlife of the area, including a comparison with a completely different catchment area.
(3) Why living things migrate, the history of migration, etc.
(4) Hostile and non-hostile environments.
(5) How different environments affect the skills and information necessary for survival.

Clearly, such an approach does the purely environmental job, in that it should raise awareness of the importance of maintaining species through preservation of their habitats. The community education orientation keeps it relevant to the lives of the children concerned and therefore, perhaps, increases a commitment to learning. The fact that parents would be learning alongside the children and teachers enhances this aspect and provides opportunities for continuing education for all the adults involved. Urban life skills would be discussed, migration of humans better understood and information about, and sensitivity to, other human cultures in the neighbourhood developed. In closely linking human migration with that of other species we are making a very important point concerning general survival.

Education **for** the environment appears to be, basically, about survival.

Many would see it as the central theme of environmental education, some appear to see it as the only theme. It is in this area in which environmental considerations can most fall into the trap of being too far removed from the concerns of the target group. Classes of eleven year olds may work hard on a 'Save the Whale' project in an area where parents are deeply concerned about saving their children from racist attacks, gang violence and substance abuse. In a leafy suburb pupils of a similar age may know all about the swan being a protected species but do not know anything about the Children Act. Even the most aware may suddenly realize that they are teaching children in Notting Hill about tea plantations and the wheatfields of Canada, whilst totally ignoring in the curriculum, their rather perilous lives in that part of London. It was the time of very bad race riots and it was the age of Rach-manism which was rife in that neighbourhood. These are lessons hard-learned but crucial!

A more effective approach might be to follow a topic called 'Survival' which would follow on quite neatly from the one on 'Migration'. As an illustration of how community education approaches guide environmental education, some aspects which might be covered are:

(1) The basic elements of survival – safe habitat, balance with other species, gaining knowledge, acquiring skills, etc.
(2) Endangered species, linking our own survival with the survival of other species. Most children and many education students answer 'No' when asked, 'Are we an endangered species?' The point to get across is that if one species is threatened then to some degree, they all are.
(3) Surviving in the neighbourhood. An inter-agency approach to the dangers of life in the catchment area and to the development of the skills, information and attitudes necessary for survival. Parents and other members of the community would also make an input.
(4) Beyond mere survival. Improving the environment, widening personal choice, helping other species and helping other members of our own species. Political implications and machinery, promotion of constructive discontent and empowerment. Compare local with other habitats.
(5) Survival of heritage. Customs, language, dialect, regional and ethnic differences in dress, food, etc. as an enrichment of the general culture and worthy of protection. Historical heritage and its survival in buildings, local memories, institutions, etc.

These suggestions are not considered to be exhaustive or to be the necessary components of such an approach. They are intended to illustrate how a community education approach typified by the four headings above, guides and coordinates environment education, linking it with the central concerns of the target group and extending it to the wider global issues.

Education **through** the environment may be considered of less importance in environmental terms. From a community education stance it is seen as using the community as a resource for the curriculum. Opportunities to use the people, places and institutions of the locality to enrich, enliven and bring relevance and realism to the curriculum are numerous and are still, relatively, unrecognized in many of our schools. Reflecting the community in the school is an important aspect of a community approach and the suggestions given above demonstrate how this can be done. Equality of opportunity provides a familiar content which validates rather than dismisses local experience. This heading also services work which may not be specifically environmental in essence.

A topic on 'Bridges' might start with a visit to one or two local bridges and end with a consideration of the effects of all the bridges within a few miles of the school falling down at the same time. A topic on 'Sources of Energy' might include a visit to the local filling station and visits from mothers or fathers employed in appropriate businesses. The local environment should continue to be used in this way so that its people, places, institutions, problems and benefits can be used to enrich and bring reality to the delivery of the everyday curriculum. This is a very important way in which the school can lower the barriers between itself and its community and lead children towards some mastery of their environment, empowerment within it, sensitivity to the different groups that make up the local community and also help develop the self-esteem and motivation needed for them to maximise their opportunities.

The approach being suggested accepts environmental education as an inherent part of community education and, seen in this way, environmental issues gain in relevance to the children, gain the support of other adults in the community served by the school, gain linkage with major movements such as equality of opportunity and multicultural education and lose some of the do-gooder, middle-class image from which they often suffer. The ultimate result of these expressions of the complex relationships discussed would be the enlistment of large numbers of previously uninvolved people in support of vital environmental causes.

Index